150 Backyard
Cookout Recipes

Gooseberry Patch

An imprint of Globe Pequot
246 Goose Lane
Guilford, CT 06437

www.gooseberrypatch.com

1•800•854•6673

Do you have a tried & true recipe...

tip, craft or memory that you'd like to see featured in
a **Gooseberry Patch** cookbook? Visit our website at
www.gooseberrypatch.com and follow the
easy steps to submit your favorite family recipe.
Or send them to us at:

Gooseberry Patch
PO Box 812
Columbus, OH 43216-0812

Don't forget to include the number of servings your recipe makes,
plus your name, address, phone number and email address. If we
select your recipe, your name will appear right along with it...
and you'll receive a **FREE** copy of the book!

Contents

Dedication

To everyone who loves cooking on the grill and
sharing backyard picnics with family & friends.
Everything just tastes better outdoors!

Chicken & Fish, Hot Off the Grill

Rich's Charcoal Lemon-Lime Chicken

Zesty with citrus flavors, this chicken is terrific for tailgating!

6 boneless, skinless chicken
   breasts
1/2 c. brown sugar, packed
1/4 c. cider vinegar
3 T. coarse mustard
juice of 1 lime
juice of 1/2 lemon

3 cloves garlic, pressed
1-1/2 t. salt, or to taste
pepper to taste
6 T. oil
Garnish: lemon slices, chopped
   fresh herbs

Place chicken in a large plastic zipping bag; set aside. In a bowl, combine remaining ingredients except oil and garnish. Blend well; whisk in oil. Add brown sugar mixture to chicken; seal bag. Refrigerate for 8 hours to overnight, turning occasionally. One hour before serving time, bring chicken to room temperature; prepare charcoal grill. Place chicken on oiled grill over medium-high heat. Grill for 4 minutes per side, or until golden and chicken juices run clear. Garnish as desired. Serves 6.

6

When you grill chicken for dinner, toss a few extra boneless, skinless chicken breasts on the grill. Slice and refrigerate to enjoy in sandwich wraps or on a salad for an easy meal with fresh-grilled flavor.

Rich's Charcoal Lemon-Lime Chicken

Grilled Basil & Tomato Chicken

Grilled Basil & Tomato Chicken

Next stop, the farmers' market, for farm-fresh chicken, ripe tomatoes and basil. Delicious!

8 roma tomatoes, divided
3/4 c. balsamic vinegar
1/4 c. fresh basil, thinly sliced
2 T. olive oil
1 clove garlic, minced
1/2 t. salt
4 boneless, skinless chicken breasts

Cut 4 tomatoes into quarters and place in a food processor; add vinegar, basil, oil, garlic and salt. Cover and process until smooth. Pour 1/2 cup of tomato mixture into a small bowl; cover and refrigerate until serving time. Pour remaining tomato mixture into a large plastic zipping bag; add chicken. Seal bag; turn to coat and refrigerate for one hour. Remove chicken from bag, discarding marinade. Grill chicken, covered, over medium heat for 4 to 6 minutes per side, until golden and juices run clear. Cut remaining tomatoes in half; grill for 2 to 3 minutes per side, until tender. Serve chicken with grilled tomatoes and reserved tomato mixture. Serves 4.

Mediterranean Herb Rub

This flavorful rub works wonders on chicken and beef. You'll want to keep a jar of it on hand for summertime grilling!

1/3 c. grated Parmesan cheese
1/3 c. pepper
2 T. dried thyme
2 T. dried rosemary
2 T. dried basil
1 t. garlic powder
1 t. salt

Mix together Parmesan cheese and pepper; add remaining ingredients and stir well. If a finer texture is desired, process in a food processor. Store in an airtight container up to one week. To use, rub over chicken or beef; grill as desired. Makes one cup.

Dijon Chicken & Fresh Herbs

*Wondering what to do with a garden full of fresh herbs? Try this...
your family will love it!*

4 to 6 boneless, skinless chicken
   breasts
1 t. kosher salt
1 t. pepper

3 to 4 T. Dijon mustard
2 T. fresh rosemary, minced
2 T. fresh thyme, minced
2 T. fresh parsley, minced

Sprinkle chicken with salt and pepper. Grill over medium-high heat 5 to
6 minutes per side, or until juices run clear. Remove from grill and brush
both sides with mustard; sprinkle with herbs. Serves 4 to 6.

Charcoal or gas? Every cookout chef has her own definite opinion. A
good rule of thumb is charcoal is for taste, gas is for haste.

Dijon Chicken & Fresh Herbs

Herbed Shrimp Tacos

Herbed Shrimp Tacos

Delicious, and so easy to whip up...why go out for tacos?

juice of 1 lime
1/2 c. plus 1 T. fresh cilantro,
  chopped and divided
1/8 t. dried thyme
1/8 t. dried oregano
1 t. salt
1/2 t. pepper
1 lb. uncooked medium shrimp,
  peeled and cleaned

1/2 c. green or red cabbage,
  shredded
1/2 c. red onion, chopped
1/2 c. radishes, shredded
4 to 6 skewers
10 6-inch flour tortillas, warmed
Garnish: guacamole

In a large plastic zipping bag, combine lime juice, one tablespoon cilantro, herbs, salt and pepper; mix well. Add shrimp; toss to coat well. Seal bag and refrigerate for at least 4 hours, turning bag once or twice. In a bowl, combine vegetables and remaining cilantro; set aside. Thread shrimp onto skewers, discarding marinade. Place skewers on a medium-hot grill. Cook until pink and cooked through, turning once or twice. Arrange shrimp in warm tortillas; garnish with guacamole and cabbage mixture. Serves 4 to 6.

13

Shrimp kabobs won't slip and twirl if the skewer is inserted through both sides of each shrimp.

Enchilada-Stuffed Poblanos

Mexican food hot off the grill! Serve with cheesy rice and tortilla chips for a delicious meal.

2-1/2 c. cooked chicken, shredded
15-oz. can black beans, drained
   and rinsed
11-oz. can corn, drained
10-oz. can diced tomatoes and
   green chiles, drained
10-oz. can enchilada sauce
1 t. salt
2 c. shredded Mexican-blend
   cheese, divided
6 poblano peppers, halved
   lengthwise and seeded

In a large bowl, combine chicken, beans, corn, tomatoes, enchilada sauce, salt and 1-1/2 cups cheese. Fill pepper halves evenly with chicken mixture. Wrap each half loosely in aluminum foil. Grill over medium-high heat for about 20 minutes, until heated through and peppers are tender. Unwrap; sprinkle with remaining cheese and let stand several minutes, until cheese is melted. Serves 6.

Toss a few whole jalapeño peppers on the grill alongside tonight's dinner for a tasty garnish.

Enchilada-Stuffed Poblanos

Hawaiian Chicken Kabobs

Hawaiian Chicken Kabobs

Light the tiki torches! This is the perfect recipe for grilling out with family & friends on a balmy summer night.

15-1/4 oz. can pineapple chunks in juice, drained and 1/2 c. juice reserved
1-1/2 lbs. boneless, skinless chicken breasts, cut into 1-inch cubes
1 lb. bacon, each slice cut into thirds

1 red or green pepper, cut into 1-inch squares
12 mushrooms
18 cherry tomatoes
6 skewers
cooked rice

Prepare Marinade, using reserved pineapple juice; refrigerate pineapple chunks. Place chicken in a large shallow glass dish. Pour marinade over chicken; cover and chill for at least one hour. Drain, pouring marinade into a small saucepan; bring to a boil for 3 minutes. Wrap each chicken cube in a piece of bacon. Thread ingredients onto skewers, alternating chicken, pineapple and vegetables. Grill skewers over medium to medium-high heat for 10 to 15 minutes, brushing often with marinade, until chicken juices run clear. Serve skewers over cooked rice. Makes 6 servings.

Marinade:

reserved 1/2 c. pineapple juice
1/2 c. soy sauce
1/4 c. canola oil
1 T. brown sugar, packed

2 t. ground ginger
1 t. garlic powder
1 t. dry mustard
1/4 t. pepper

In a small saucepan, stir together all ingredients. Bring to a boil over medium heat; reduce heat and simmer for 5 minutes. Cool slightly.

Use a grill basket to cook small pieces of meat, fish and veggies. They won't fall through the grate and are much easier to turn for even cooking.

Brandie's Chicken Skewers

A flavorful marinade made with ingredients you probably already have in the kitchen. Toss a salad and dinner is served.

1 c. olive oil
3/4 c. soy sauce
1/2 c. lemon juice
1/4 c. mustard
1/4 c. Worcestershire sauce

2 t. garlic, minced
1-1/2 t. pepper
6 boneless, skinless chicken
  breasts, cut into 1-inch strips
4 skewers

In a bowl, mix all ingredients except chicken. If desired, process mixture in a blender until smooth. Place chicken in a shallow glass dish; add marinade and turn to coat well. Cover and refrigerate for 4 hours to overnight. Drain, discarding marinade. Thread chicken onto skewers. Grill over medium to medium-high heat for 5 minutes per side, or until chicken juices run clear. Serves 4.

Super-Easy BBQ Chicken

Perfect for a rainy-day meal! So simple to fix in your slow cooker... just add a fresh green salad.

16 chicken drumsticks and/or
  thighs, skin removed

2 c. favorite barbecue sauce
cooked rice

Place chicken in a microwave-safe dish. Cover and microwave on high for 15 minutes. Carefully remove hot chicken to a 6-quart slow cooker, spooning some barbecue sauce over each piece. Cover and cook on low setting for 6 to 8 hours, until chicken is very tender. Discard bones. Serve chicken and sauce over cooked rice. Serves 6 to 8.

For evenly cooked kabobs, leave a little space between the pieces on the skewers.

Brandie's Chicken Skewers

Grilled Chicken with White BBQ Sauce

Grilled Chicken with White BBQ Sauce

Grilled chicken with a spicy rub and a creamy sauce...you're going to love it! Be sure to allow enough time for the chicken to marinate.

3 lbs. chicken thighs and drumsticks	1 T. paprika
1 T. dried thyme	1 t. onion powder
1 T. dried oregano	1 t. salt
1 T. ground cumin	1/2 t. pepper

Pat chicken dry with paper towels; set aside. Combine seasonings in a bowl; rub mixture evenly over chicken. Place chicken in a large plastic zipping bag. Seal and chill 4 hours. Make White BBQ Sauce at least 2 hours ahead of serving time; refrigerate. Shortly before serving time, remove chicken from bag, discarding bag. Grill chicken, covered, over medium-high heat for 8 to 10 minutes per side, until crisp, golden and chicken juices run clear when pierced. Serve chicken with sauce. Serves 4 to 6.

21

White BBQ Sauce:

1-1/2 c. mayonnaise	2 t. prepared horseradish
1/4 c. white wine vinegar	1 t. sugar
1 clove garlic, minced	1/2 t. salt
1 T. spicy brown mustard	1 T. pepper

Stir together all ingredients. Cover and refrigerate for at least 2 hours.

Using jute, bundle together fresh herbs like rosemary, thyme or marjoram to create an herb basting brush...it really adds flavor to grilled foods.

Baja Fish Tacos

Serve these tacos with black beans on the side for the perfect quick & easy meal!

2 c. green or red cabbage, shredded
3 T. lime juice, divided
2 t. olive oil
1/3 c. fresh cilantro, chopped and
   divided
1 t. chili powder
1-1/4 lbs. mahi-mahi fillets,
   3/4-inch thick

8 8-inch corn tortillas, warmed
1 avocado, halved, pitted and
   thinly sliced
1/4 c. radishes, sliced
Garnish: sour cream, salsa

In a bowl, toss cabbage with one tablespoon lime juice; set aside. In a shallow dish, mix oil, remaining lime juice, one tablespoon cilantro and chili powder. Add fish fillets to oil mixture; turn to coat all sides. Let stand for 10 minutes. Place fish on a lightly greased grill over medium heat. Cook for 5 to 7 minutes, turning once, just until fish flakes easily. Remove fish to a plate; break into chunks. Fill each tortilla with fish, cabbage, avocado, radishes and remaining cilantro. Top with sour cream and salsa. Serves 4 to 5.

Whip up a speedy black bean salad. Combine one cup drained and rinsed black beans, 1/2 cup corn, 1/2 cup salsa and 1/4 teaspoon cumin or chili powder. Chill until serving time...tasty!

Baja Fish Tacos

Best Friends' Greek Pasta

Best Friends' Greek Pasta

Looking for something a little different from the grill?
This dish is a snap to make.

16-oz. pkg. penne pasta, uncooked
3 to 4 boneless, skinless chicken
   breasts
Cajun seasoning to taste
1/4 c. basil pesto sauce
2 T. garlic, minced

6-oz. jar Kalamata olives, drained
   and coarsely chopped
3/4 c. cherry tomatoes, coarsely
   chopped
8-oz. pkg. crumbled feta cheese
3/4 c. Italian salad dressing

Cook pasta according to package directions; drain. Meanwhile, sprinkle chicken with seasoning. Grill chicken over medium heat until juices run clear when pierced. Slice chicken into bite-size pieces and set aside. While pasta is still hot, stir in pesto and garlic; mix well. Stir in chicken, olives, tomatoes and cheese. Add salad dressing to coat; mix well. Serve warm or cooled. Serves 4 to 6.

Pick up some pint-size Mason jars...perfect for serving frosty cold beverages at casual get-togethers.

Italian Chicken in Foil

So easy to put together...let everyone fix their own packets.

1 boneless, skinless chicken breast
   or thigh
1 potato, peeled and cut lengthwise
   into 1/8-inch slices
1 zucchini, sliced 1/4-inch thick

salt to taste
3 jumbo black olives
2 t. tomato sauce
1/2 t. dried oregano
1 t. butter, diced

Season chicken, potato and zucchini with salt; set aside. Layer potato and zucchini slices on an 18-inch piece of heavy-duty aluminum foil. Top with chicken, olives, tomato sauce and oregano; dot with butter. Wrap securely in foil. Grill packet over medium heat for 25 to 30 minutes on each side, or until chicken juices run clear and vegetables are tender. Makes one serving.

Kid-Friendly Grilled Chicken

Your kids will love this one, and so will you. It's so flavorful,
yet simple to make.

1/2 c. Italian salad dressing
1 T. honey

1 t. lime juice
1 lb. chicken tenders

Mix salad dressing, honey and lime juice in a bowl. Add chicken; cover and refrigerate for 3 to 8 hours. Drain, discarding marinade. Grill chicken over medium heat for 3 to 4 minutes per side, until golden and juices run clear. Makes 4 servings.

For the juiciest grilled foods, flip burgers using a spatula,
but don't press them down on the grill. Turn steaks,
chicken and brats with tongs.

Italian Chicken in Foil

Rebecca's Campfire Packets

Rebecca's Campfire Packets

Delicious and a breeze to put together. Smoked chicken sausages come in lots of great flavors...we like chicken & apple!

4 to 6 redskin potatoes, thinly
  sliced
1 green pepper, thinly sliced into
  strips
1 onion, sliced
2 T. olive oil

2 T. steak seasoning salt
salt and pepper to taste
Optional: 1 T. garlic, minced
4 smoked chicken sausage links,
  sliced into bite-size pieces

Spray 18-inch pieces of aluminum foil with non-stick vegetable spray. Divide potatoes, pepper and onion evenly among foil pieces. Drizzle with olive oil; sprinkle with seasonings and garlic, if using. Arrange sausage slices on top. Wrap foil securely to form packages; place on a grill over medium heat. Cook for 14 to 18 minutes, turning packages once, until hot and potatoes are tender. Makes 4 servings.

Sweet-and-Sour Chicken

29

Foil packet meals are a great way to cook out...let the family help! Serve over cooked rice and top with crunchy chow mein noodles.

4 boneless, skinless chicken
  breasts or thighs
8-oz. can pineapple chunks,
  drained

1 green pepper, thinly sliced
1/4 onion, thinly sliced
1 c. sweet-and-sour sauce, divided

On an 18-inch piece of heavy-duty aluminum foil, place one chicken piece, 1/4 each of pineapple, pepper and onion, and one tablespoon sauce. May drizzle with a little more sauce. Fold over foil; seal edges to make a packet. Repeat to make 3 more packets. Grill packets, covered, over medium heat for 15 to 20 minutes, until chicken juices run clear. May also bake packets on baking sheets at 350 degrees for 35 to 45 minutes. Serves 4.

Heavy-duty aluminum foil is perfect for making grilling packets. It seals well and resists tearing.

April's Barbecue Chicken

Use this delicious sauce on everything from ribs to pulled pork.

3 lbs. chicken, or 6 bone-in chicken breasts

1 T. garlic powder
1 t. onion powder

Place chicken in a large stockpot over medium-high heat. Cover with water; stir in garlic powder and onion powder. Bring to a boil. Reduce heat; cover and cook for about 15 minutes. Meanwhile, make Barbecue Sauce. Place chicken on an oiled grate over medium-high heat. Grill for 30 to 40 minutes, turning and basting often with barbecue sauce, until chicken juices run clear. Makes 6 to 8 servings.

Barbecue Sauce:

2 c. catsup
1 to 2 c. brown sugar, packed and divided
1/2 t. dry mustard

1/2 t. chili powder
1 t. garlic powder
1/2 t. onion powder
1 t. smoke-flavored cooking sauce

In a saucepan over medium heat, mix together catsup, one cup brown sugar, mustard and seasonings. Add remaining brown sugar to taste. Simmer about 15 minutes; add smoke-flavored sauce and cook another few minutes.

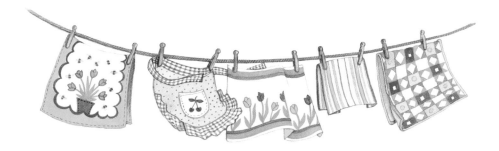

Vintage tea towels make whimsical oversized napkins...so handy for messy-but-tasty foods like barbecued ribs, buttered corn on the cob and juicy wedges of watermelon.

April's Barbecue Chicken

Low-Country Shrimp B

Low-Country Shrimp Boil

Carry the pot out to the backyard picnic table when it's done! So much fun...how often do you get to eat your whole meal with your hands?

6 qts. water
3/4 c. seafood seasoning
2 lbs. new redskin potatoes
2 lbs. smoked pork sausage, cut
    into 1-inch pieces
5 ears sweet corn, husked and
    halved

2 lbs. uncooked large shrimp,
    cleaned
Garnish: cocktail sauce, melted
    butter, lemon wedges

Combine water and seasoning in a large pot; bring to a boil. Add potatoes and boil, covered, for 15 minutes. Add sausage and continue to boil for 5 minutes. Add corn; boil for another 5 minutes. Add shrimp and boil until shrimp are pink, about 4 minutes. Drain and transfer mixture to a large serving bowl. Garnish as desired. Serves 6 to 8.

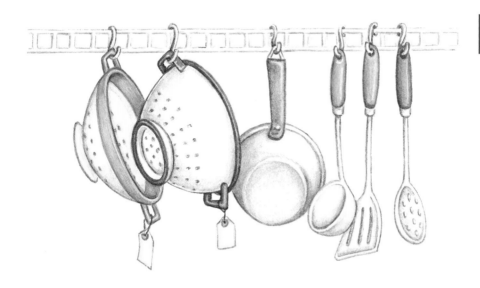

33

Cover the picnic table with brown paper for a warm-weather meal... afterwards, just roll it up and toss away! Perfect for peel & eat shrimp, fried chicken and other tasty-but-messy suppers.

Chicken & Fish, Hot Off the Grill

Lakeside Fish & Veggies

Make this all-in-one supper with the catch of the day...
it's easy to prepare and so delicious.

1 lb. fish fillets, 1/2-inch thick
2 cloves garlic, minced
1 lemon, peeled, sliced and seeded
1/2 t. dill weed
1/4 t. dry mustard

2 T. butter, diced and divided
3 potatoes, peeled and thinly sliced
16 baby carrots
1 stalk celery, thinly sliced
1/8 t. salt

Lightly grease one side of a 24-inch piece of aluminum foil. Arrange fish fillets in the center of foil; sprinkle with garlic and arrange lemon slices over top. Sprinkle with dill weed and mustard. Dot with one tablespoon butter. Arrange vegetables around fish. Dot with remaining butter; season with salt. Fold aluminum foil around fish and vegetables, sealing well. Place packets on a grill over medium-high heat. Cook for 25 to 35 minutes, until fish flakes easily and vegetables are tender. Makes 4 servings.

34 Cucumber Dill Sauce

A cool, refreshing sauce that's especially tasty spooned over salmon, shrimp and steak...even grilled vegetables.

1 cucumber, peeled and divided
8-oz. container sour cream
1 T. fresh dill, chopped, or
   1 t. dill weed

zest and juice of 1 lemon
1 t. sugar
salt and pepper to taste

Grate 1/4 of the cucumber into a bowl; set aside. Cut remaining cucumber into 1/2-inch cubes and add to grated cucumber. Stir in remaining ingredients; mix thoroughly. Cover and chill until ready to serve, about 30 minutes. Makes 10 to 12 servings.

If people concentrated on the really important things in life, there'd be a shortage of fishing poles.
-Doug Larson

Lakeside Fish & Veggies

Buttermilk Fried Chicken

Buttermilk Fried Chicken

Serve this crisp and delicious chicken hot, or tuck it in the cooler to enjoy cold...either way, it's sure to be a hit.

2-1/2 lbs. chicken	1-1/2 t. salt
1 c. buttermilk	1/2 t. pepper
1 c. all-purpose flour	oil for frying

Combine chicken pieces and buttermilk in a large bowl. Cover and refrigerate for one hour. Meanwhile, combine flour, salt and pepper in a large plastic zipping bag. Drain chicken, discarding buttermilk. Working in batches, add chicken to bag and toss to coat. Shake off excess flour and let chicken rest for 15 minutes. Heat 1/4 inch of oil in a large skillet over medium heat. Fry chicken in oil until golden on all sides. Reduce heat to medium-low; cover and simmer, turning occasionally, for 40 to 45 minutes, until juices run clear. Uncover and cook 5 minutes longer. Serves 4 to 6.

37

Serve fried chicken in clean new paper buckets from the local paint store, just for fun. Lined with red-checked paper napkins, they're easy to toss when the picnic is over.

Tangy BBQ Chicken

*Coffee lovers will like this chicken grilled with a coffee-based sauce.
The recipe makes about 1-1/2 cups of the sauce...
it's tasty on chicken, beef and pork.*

1 c. brewed coffee
1 c. catsup
1/2 c. sugar
1/2 c. Worcestershire sauce

1/4 c. cider vinegar
1/8 t. pepper
8 chicken thighs and drumsticks

In a saucepan, combine all ingredients except chicken. Bring to a boil over medium heat; reduce heat to low. Simmer, uncovered, for 30 to 35 minutes until thickened, stirring occasionally. Grill chicken as desired, brushing with sauce as it cooks. Makes 8 servings.

Smoky Mountain Barbecue Sauce

*Scrumptious on grilled chicken...just add corn on the cob
and your meal is complete!*

1/4 c. oil
1/2 c. onion, chopped
1 clove garlic, minced
1 c. tomato purée
1 c. water

1/4 c. brown sugar, packed
1/4 c. cider vinegar
1 T. chili powder
3 whole cloves
1 bay leaf

Heat oil in a skillet over medium heat. Add onion and garlic; cook until onion is clear. Add remaining ingredients; simmer until brown sugar is dissolved and sauce has thickened. Discard bay leaf and cloves, if desired. Cover and refrigerate if not used immediately. Makes about 2-1/2 cups.

Tangy BBQ Chicken

Tomato-Mushroom Grilled Fish

Tomato-Mushroom Grilled Fish

A wonderful summer recipe-for-two! Baking in parchment paper or foil packets makes clean-up a breeze. Try it with orange roughy, sea bass or halibut.

1 T. butter, softened	1/2 c. sliced mushrooms
4 c. baby spinach	1 tomato, chopped
2 6-oz. white fish fillets, 1/2-inch thick	2 T. lime juice
	1 T. olive oil
salt and pepper	4 sprigs fresh thyme
1/2 c. zucchini, cut into thin slivers	

For each packet, layer 3 sheets of parchment paper or two 15-inch pieces of aluminum foil. Spread softened butter down the center of each top piece. Divide spinach evenly, placing it on the buttered area; arrange fish fillets on top. Season with salt and pepper. Divide zucchini, mushrooms and tomato evenly over fish. Drizzle with lime juice and oil; top with thyme sprigs. Fold one long edge of paper or foil over the other; tuck short ends underneath, sealing tightly. Place packets on a grill over medium-high heat. Cook for 15 to 18 minutes, until fish flakes easily. Makes 2 servings.

Dijon-Grilled Fish

Flavorful fish for a lighter summer meal...great for guests who aren't burger fans. Toss some veggies on the other side of the grill to round out the menu.

1 lb. orange roughy fillets	2 T. lemon juice
1/2 c. butter	1 t. seasoned salt
2 T. Dijon mustard	Garnish: paprika

Place fish fillets in a shallow dish; set aside. Combine butter, mustard, lemon juice and salt in a small saucepan; simmer over low heat for 10 minutes. Let cool; spoon over fish. Cover and refrigerate for 30 minutes. Grill fish over medium heat for 3 to 6 minutes on each side, basting with remaining sauce. Sprinkle with paprika at serving time. Makes 4 servings.

Grilled Tilapia with Pineapple Salsa

Treat yourself to this wonderful recipe when fresh pineapple is in season... it's out-of-this-world good!

1 T. canola oil
2 T. lime juice
1/4 t. salt

1/8 t. pepper
2 lbs. tilapia fillets

Make Pineapple Salsa ahead of time; chill. In a small bowl, combine oil and lime juice. Brush over fillets; sprinkle with salt and pepper. Cook fish on a grill pan over medium heat, turning once, for 6 to 8 minutes, until fish flakes easily with a fork. Serve fish topped with Pineapple Salsa. Serves 6 to 8.

Pineapple Salsa:

2 c. pineapple, diced
2 green onions, chopped
1/4 c. green pepper, diced
1/4 c. fresh cilantro, minced

4 t. lime juice
1/8 t. cayenne pepper
1/8 t. salt

Combine all ingredients in a small bowl. Mix well; cover and chill until serving time.

How can you tell when a pineapple is ripe? Just check the base...if it's green, it's not ripe yet. If it's orange or mushy, it's too ripe. But if it's yellow and bright, it's just right.

Grilled Tilapia with Pineapple Salsa

Grilled Halibut & Lemon Sauce

Grilled Halibut & Lemon Sauce

*A quick and delicious, fresh-tasting fish and sauce
that never fails to impress.*

1/4 c. dry white wine or
   chicken broth
3 T. lemon juice
1 t. dried oregano

1/2 t. salt
1/8 t. pepper
2 lbs. halibut steak, 1-inch thick

Combine all ingredients except fish into a large plastic zipping bag; mix well. Add fish to bag; turn to coat. Seal bag and refrigerate for 30 minutes to 2 hours. Make Lemon Sauce; set aside. Drain marinade into a small saucepan; bring to a boil for 3 minutes. Place fish on a lightly oiled grill over medium heat. Grill for 10 to 12 minutes, turning once and brushing with reserved marinade, until fish flakes easily with a fork. Serve with Lemon Sauce. Serves 4.

Lemon Sauce:

1/4 c. olive oil
2 T. lemon juice
2 T. shallots, chopped
2 T. capers, chopped
1 T. fresh parsley, chopped

1/2 t. dry mustard
1/2 t. garlic, minced
1/4 t. salt
1/8 t. white pepper

45

Whisk together all ingredients in a small bowl.

Whip up some herbed dill butter to serve with grilled fish. Blend
2 tablespoons softened butter, 2 tablespoons lemon juice, a teaspoon
of minced garlic and a teaspoon of dried or fresh dill...heavenly!

BBQ Shrimp & Pineapple Kabobs

Delightfully different from the usual steak or chicken kabobs, with a tropical taste that's sure to make you feel like you're soaking in the sun.

8 uncooked large shrimp, peeled
    and cleaned
1 c. pineapple, cubed
1 green pepper, cut into 2-inch
    squares

1 sweet or red onion, cut
    into wedges
teriyaki barbecue sauce to taste
cooked rice

Thread shrimp, pineapple, green pepper and onion pieces alternately onto 4 skewers. Place kabobs on a lightly oiled grill pan over medium heat. Cook for 8 to 10 minutes, turning and brushing frequently with barbecue sauce, until shrimp are pink and cooked through. Serve kabobs over cooked rice. Makes 4 servings.

Sweet & Easy Salmon

46

So easy! Simple to whip up, with a short marinating time and a quick grill time.

2 T. butter
2 T. brown sugar, packed
1 to 2 cloves garlic, minced
1 T. lemon juice

2 t. soy sauce
1/2 t. pepper
4 salmon fillets

Combine all ingredients except salmon fillets in a small saucepan. Cook and stir over medium until sugar is dissolved; cool. Place fillets in a shallow glass dish; pour cooled marinade over top. Let stand for 10 to 15 minutes. Remove salmon from dish. Spray grill with non-stick vegetable spray and grill over medium heat for 4 to 5 minutes on each side, basting occasionally with marinade. Discard any remaining marinade. Serves 4.

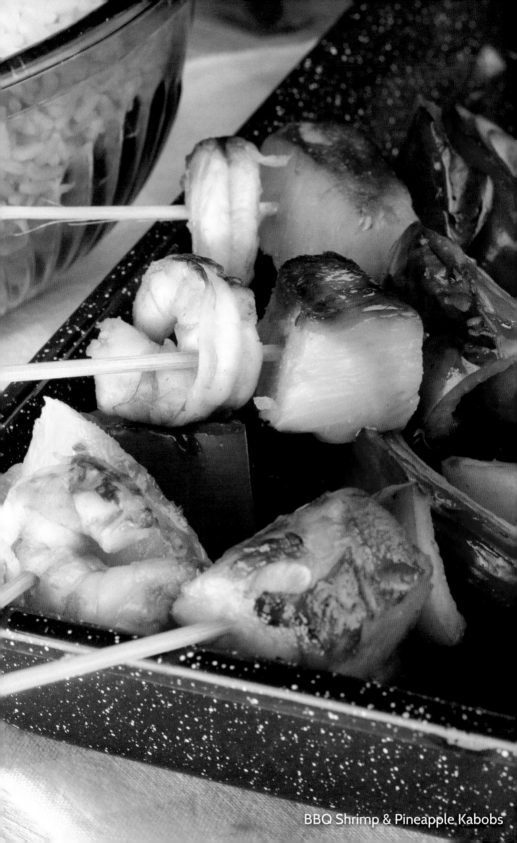

BBQ Shrimp & Pineapple Kabobs

Here's an easy way to tell if the grill is ready to cook. If you can hold your hand comfortably 5 inches over the grill:

- for 5 to 6 seconds = low heat, or 250 to 300 degrees
- for 4 seconds = medium heat, or 350 to 400 degrees
- for 2 seconds = high heat, or 400 to 450 degrees

 Freezing extra pieces of chicken from a family pack? Add a flavorful marinade to plastic zipping bags of uncooked chicken and freeze. When you thaw it for cooking, the chicken will be deliciously seasoned. So convenient!

 Make frozen fish taste fresh-caught. Just place the frozen fillets in a shallow dish, cover with milk and thaw in the refrigerator overnight. Drain well and pat dry before grilling.

 Crisp coleslaw pairs well with grilled chicken and fish. Perk up your favorite coleslaw with some mandarin oranges or pineapple tidbits for a delicious change.

Juicy Steak & BBQ Pork

Asian Flank Steak

You'll really like the flavor of this steak. Serve with seasoned rice and steamed snow peas for a wonderful meal.

2 to 3-lb. beef flank steak
3/4 c. soy sauce
1/4 c. sesame oil
2 T. sake wine or white vinegar

2 to 3 green onions, thinly sliced
2 cloves garlic, minced
2 t. sugar

Lightly score steak diagonally on both sides; set aside. Combine remaining ingredients in a shallow glass dish. Add steak; turn to coat. Cover and refrigerate up to 8 hours. Drain, discarding marinade. Grill steak over medium-high heat to desired doneness, about 10 minutes per side, reducing heat to medium if cooking too fast. Let steak stand for 10 minutes; slice thinly against the grain. Makes 6 to 8 servings.

Trim excess fat from steaks and chops before grilling to cut down on flare-ups. A squirt bottle of water is handy for putting out flames.

Asian Flank Steak

Teriyaki BBQ Beef

Teriyaki BBQ Beef

This scrumptious recipe has stood the test of time! Serve the skewers on cooked rice or scoop the beef strips into buns to serve.

1/2 c. soy sauce
1/2-inch piece fresh ginger, peeled
  and grated
2 T. sugar

1 clove garlic, crushed
3 lbs. beef tri-tip or flank steak,
  thinly sliced into strips
8 skewers

In a large glass dish, combine sauce, ginger, sugar and garlic. Add beef; cover and refrigerate at least 30 minutes. Drain, discarding marinade. Thread beef strips onto skewers. Grill over medium heat to desired doneness, about 5 to 10 minutes, turning once or twice. Serves 8 to 10.

Safety first! Be sure to place grilled food on a clean plate, never on a plate that previously held uncooked food.

Ribs with Espresso Barbecue Sauce

Ribs and barbecue sauce can be prepared one day ahead. Just cool slightly, cover separately and refrigerate.

2 T. Mexican-style hot chili powder
1 T. paprika
1 T. ground cumin
1-1/2 t. salt
3/4 t. pepper
4 lbs. baby back pork ribs, cut into serving-size pieces
12-oz. bottle dark beer

Whisk seasonings together in a small bowl to blend; rub mixture over ribs. Place ribs in a large heavy roasting pan; set aside. In a large saucepan, bring beer to a boil over medium heat; cook until reduced to one cup, about 5 minutes. Pour beer around ribs; cover tightly with aluminum foil. Bake at 400 degrees until fork-tender, about 1-1/2 hours. Meanwhile, prepare Espresso Barbecue Sauce. When ribs are tender, brush with sauce; grill over medium heat for 3 minutes. Turn ribs; brush again with sauce and grill for an additional 3 to 4 minutes, until heated through. Bring remaining sauce to a boil; serve with ribs. Makes 4 to 6 servings.

Espresso Barbecue Sauce:

18-oz. bottle favorite barbecue sauce
1/2 c. water
2 T. brown sugar, packed
1 T. instant coffee granules

Combine all ingredients in a saucepan over medium heat. Simmer until slightly thickened, stirring occasionally, about 10 minutes.

Host a tailgating cook-off. Invite everyone to bring their own game-day specialty like BBQ ribs or chicken wings. You provide the beverages, baskets of warm cornbread and plenty of napkins. Have a prize for the winner!

Ribs with Espresso Barbecue Sauce

Kansas City Pork Chops

Kansas City Pork Chops

These grilled pork chops will make your backyard smell like a smokin' barbecue joint. They are bursting with flavor and so easy!

1/4 c. brown sugar, packed
2 T. paprika
1-1/2 t. garlic powder
1-1/2 t. chili powder
1-1/2 t. onion powder

1-1/2 t. salt
1-1/2 t. pepper
4 center-cut pork loin chops
favorite barbecue sauce to taste

Mix together brown sugar and seasonings in a small bowl. Place pork chops in a plastic zipping bag; sprinkle mixture over chops. Close bag tightly and toss to coat pork chops. Refrigerate at least 2 hours. Place pork chops on an oiled grill over medium-high heat; grill for 3 minutes per side. Reduce heat to low; continue cooking for about 7 minutes per side, until pork juices run clear. During the last 2 minutes on each side, baste with barbecue sauce. Remove from heat; baste with a little extra sauce before serving. Makes 4 servings.

Barbecued Pork Chops

Chances are, you already have the ingredients in your pantry for this savory marinade.

8 bone-in pork chops
1/2 c. honey
1/3 c. soy sauce

2/3 c. hot water
garlic powder to taste

Arrange pork chops in a shallow glass dish; set aside. In a small bowl, stir together remaining ingredients; spoon over chops. Cover and refrigerate overnight for 2 to 8 hours. Drain, discarding marinade. Arrange chops on grill over medium heat and cook for about 10 minutes on each side, depending on thickness of chops. May also be placed on a broiler pan; broil for about 10 minutes per side. Makes 8 servings.

For the most mouthwatering marinated chops and steaks, pat the meat dry with a paper towel after draining off the marinade. Sprinkle on any seasonings before placing it on the hot grill.

German Spiesbraten

This overnight dish is a perfect idea for a cookout if you're looking for something a little different.

3 T. salt
2 t. pepper
1-1/2 T. paprika
1-1/2 T. celery salt
1 T. garlic powder

4 t. meat tenderizer
2 onions, thinly sliced
5-lb. pork tenderloin, cut into
   serving-size pieces
12 pretzel rolls, split

Combine all spices and tenderizer in a small bowl; set aside. Alternately layer onion and pork pieces in a deep glass dish, sprinkling evenly with seasoning mixture after each layer. Cover and refrigerate for 24 hours. Grill pork and onion over medium heat until pork is no longer pink in the center and onion is tender. Slice pork; fill split rolls with pork and onion slices. Makes 12 servings.

A ridged cast-iron grill skillet is handy for grilling on your stovetop whenever it's too cold or rainy to use the grill outdoors.

German Spiesbraten

Sweet-Hot Ribeye Steak

Sweet-Hot Ribeye Steak

Just add baked potatoes and a big tossed salad...yum!

1-lb. boneless beef ribeye steak
2 cloves garlic, pressed
2 t. water
2 T. sweet-hot mustard

1 t. fresh rosemary, chopped
1/2 t. fresh thyme, chopped
salt and pepper to taste

Place steak in a shallow dish; set aside. Combine garlic and water in a microwave-safe dish; microwave on high setting for 30 seconds. Stir in mustard and seasonings; brush mixture on both sides of steak. Grill over medium-high heat to desired doneness, about 12 minutes for medium. Slice into portions for serving. Makes 2 to 4 servings.

Chimichurri Sauce

Serve this traditional green herb sauce from Argentina with grilled beef, chicken or fish. It's a delicious way to use fresh herbs from your garden.

1-1/2 c. fresh flat-leaf parsley, packed
3/4 c. extra-virgin olive oil
3 T. white wine vinegar

2 T. fresh oregano, chopped
6 cloves garlic, quartered
1/4 t. red pepper flakes
salt and pepper to taste

Combine all ingredients in a food processor; process until smooth. Use immediately. May be refrigerated up to 4 hours; bring to room temperature at serving time. Makes 4 servings.

Remove grilled steak to a platter and let stand for 10 to 15 minutes before slicing and serving..it'll be nice and juicy!

Angie's Hobo Dinner

An old camping favorite that's fun at home too. It's quick, delicious and so easy the kids can help assemble it.

1-1/2 lbs. ground beef
1 to 2 T. Worcestershire sauce
1/2 t. seasoned pepper
1/2 t. dried basil
1/8 t. garlic powder

4 redskin potatoes, sliced
4 carrots, peeled and sliced
1 c. sliced mushrooms
1 onion, sliced
olive oil and dried parsley to taste

In a bowl, combine beef, Worcestershire sauce and seasonings. Mix well and form into 4 to 6 patties. Place each patty on an 18-inch piece of heavy-duty aluminum foil. Top patties evenly with vegetables. Drizzle with olive oil; sprinkle with parsley. Seal foil packets. Grill packets over medium heat, or cook on hot campfire coals, for 15 to 20 minutes per side. May also place packets on baking sheets; bake at 375 degrees for about one hour. Serves 4 to 6.

Grilling foil-wrapped dinners tonight? Let the kids help put them together. They can mix & match their favorite veggies, meats and flavors just as they like.

Angie's Hobo Dinner

Evelyn's Grilled Pork Loin

Evelyn's Grilled Pork Loin

Serve with rice pilaf and fresh summer vegetables...delicious!

3-lb. boneless pork loin roast
1 c. soy sauce
1/2 c. sherry or apple juice
1 t. mustard

1 t. ground ginger
1/2 t. salt
1/4 t. garlic powder

Place roast in a shallow glass dish. Combine remaining ingredients in a bowl and pour over roast. Cover and refrigerate for 2 hours to overnight. Drain marinade into a small saucepan; bring to a boil for 3 minutes. Place roast on a grill over medium-high heat, 6 to 8 inches above heat. Grill, covered, for 1-1/2 to 2 hours, turning and brushing with marinade every 30 minutes. Slice roast thinly to serve. Serves 6 to 8.

Mike's Grill Surprise

A great one-dish summer meal! Play a game of softball or simply relax in the shade while dinner cooks.

2 lbs. Polish sausage or pork
  tenderloin, cut into bite-size
  pieces
6 to 8 new redskin potatoes,
  quartered

4 c. fresh green beans, snapped
12-oz. can regular or
  non-alcoholic beer
1 c. butter, sliced
salt and lemon pepper to taste

Place sausage or tenderloin in a large disposable roaster; surround with potatoes and green beans. Pour beer over all; dot with butter and sprinkle with seasonings. Add enough water to fill roaster 1/4 full. Cover with aluminum foil. Place roaster on a grill over medium heat. Cook for 1-1/2 to 2 hours; check after one hour and add more water if needed. Serves 6 to 8.

Picnic in a Pan

Like a summer fellowship picnic in a dish! Feel free to add other favorite veggies too.

4 potatoes, peeled and cubed
4 ears sweet corn, broken in half
4 tomatoes, sliced
4 green peppers, sliced
1/2 lb. whole mushrooms, trimmed
  and halved

1 lb. smoked pork sausage,
  quartered
1/2 c. butter, sliced
1/2 c. water
1/2 c. Worcestershire sauce
seasoned salt to taste

Layer vegetables and sausage on a 24-inch piece of heavy-duty aluminum foil. Dot with butter. Drizzle with water and Worcestershire sauce. Add seasoned salt to taste. Fold up sides of foil; seal into a packet. Grill over medium heat for about one hour, until vegetables are tender. Serves 4.

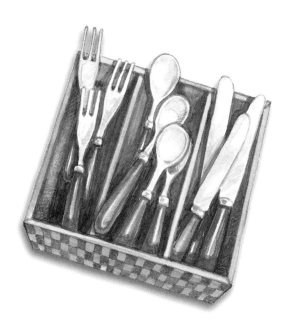

It's a lovely thing...everyone sitting down together, sharing food.
-Alice May Brock

Picnic in a Pan

Mitchell's Wonderful Brisket

Mitchell's Wonderful Brisket

Treat your family & friends to this amazing brisket. It bakes in the oven for several hours, giving you plenty of time to relax and enjoy your guests.

5-lb. beef brisket
1 t. garlic powder
salt and pepper to taste
1 onion, sliced
1 bay leaf
10 to 12 whole cloves

3/4 c. chili sauce
1 T. Worcestershire sauce
1/2 c. water
1/4 c. brown sugar, packed
1/2 t. paprika

Season brisket on all sides with garlic powder, salt and pepper. Place in an ungreased 13"x9" baking pan. Lay sliced onion and bay leaf on top of brisket. Cover with aluminum foil and refrigerate for 2 to 3 hours. Bake brisket, covered, at 300 degrees for 3 hours. Remove from oven; stick cloves evenly into brisket. In a bowl, combine remaining ingredients. Stir to mix well; spoon over brisket. Bake, uncovered, for one hour longer. Let stand at room temperature for several minutes; discard bay leaf and cloves. Slice to serve. Serves 10 to 12.

69

Turn your favorite sliced or shredded pork, beef or chicken barbecue into party food. Serve up bite-size sandwiches on slider buns.

Grilled Ham & Pineapple

*A delicious combination! If time is short, use canned pineapple slices,
adding them to the grill when the ham is almost done.*

1 fresh pineapple
3 T. honey
1-1/2 to 2-lb. ham steak, 1-inch
   thick
1/4 c. mustard

1/4 c. pineapple juice
2 T. brown sugar, packed
1/2 t. prepared horseradish
1/8 t. salt

Remove top of pineapple, but do not peel. Cut lengthwise into 8 wedges.
Place wedges in a pan and brush with honey. Cover and refrigerate for one
hour, turning occasionally. Place pineapple wedges skin-side down on an
oiled grill over medium-high heat. Grill for 20 minutes, or until heated
through. Cut ham steak into serving-size pieces, if desired. Mix together
remaining ingredients except ham. Grill ham, brushing often with mustard
sauce, until glazed and heated through. Cut ham into serving-size pieces;
serve with pineapple and remaining sauce for drizzling. Serves 4 to 6.

Slow-Cooked Kalua Pork

*A favorite from Hawaii...but there's no need to dig a cooking pit! Serve
with roasted sweet potatoes and fresh fruit kabobs for a memorable meal.*

4-lb. pork butt roast
4-oz. bottle smoke-flavored
   cooking sauce, divided

kosher salt to taste
cooked rice

Place pork roast in a 6-quart slow cooker. Season with salt; cover roast
generously with sauce, using 1/3 to 1/2 of the bottle. Cover and cook on
low setting for 8 hours, or on high setting for 4 hours, until very tender.
Shred pork; serve over cooked rice. Serves 8.

Grilled Ham & Pineapple

Grilled Flank Steak Sandwich

Grilled Flank Steak Sandwich

On a hot summer's evening, it's nice to keep the kitchen cool! Grill the steak in the backyard, then finish the sandwich indoors.

1 to 1-1/2 lb. beef flank steak
seasoned salt and pepper to taste
1 sweet onion, thinly sliced
1 green or red pepper, thinly sliced
2 to 3 t. olive oil

mayonnaise to taste
8 to 12 slices country-style bread
4 to 6 slices provolone cheese
softened butter to taste

Grill steak over medium heat to desired doneness. Remove from grill; add seasonings and let rest for about 10 minutes. Slice steak slice thinly on the diagonal. Meanwhile, in a skillet over medium-high heat, sauté onion and pepper in oil until onion is caramelized, about 10 minutes. Spread mayonnaise on one side of bread. Assemble sandwiches with bread, sliced steak, onion mixture and cheese slices. Spread a little butter over outside of sandwiches. Heat a countertop grill, panini press or grill pan. Grill sandwiches until toasted and cheese is melted. Makes 4 to 6 servings.

73

Steak Onion Butter

A dollop of this yummy spread makes a perfectly grilled steak even better!

1/4 c. butter, softened
1/4 c. Bermuda onion, grated
1/4 c. fresh parsley, minced
1 t. Worcestershire sauce

1/2 t. salt
1/2 t. pepper
1/4 t. dry mustard

Blend all ingredients in a small bowl. Use immediately or cover and refrigerate. Makes about 3/4 cup.

Dining outdoors on a hot, humid day? Keep salt free-flowing...simply add a few grains of rice to the shaker.

Tom's BBQ Ribs

Wonderful! You'll want to make up extra packets of this divine spice mix.

5 lbs. pork back ribs, cut into
   serving-size pieces

brown sugar barbecue sauce
   to taste

Coat both sides of ribs with Spice Mix. Wrap ribs in a double thickness of aluminum foil. Bake at 350 degrees for about 20 minutes. Preheat grill on high; turn grill down to medium. Place ribs on grill, still wrapped in foil. Cook for about one hour, turning occasionally, until tender. Remove ribs from grill. Increase grill to high heat; brush grill lightly with oil. Unwrap ribs and place on grill; brush with barbecue sauce. Cover and grill for about 5 minutes per side, brushing again with barbecue sauce, until slightly blackened. Makes 4 to 6 servings.

Spice Mix:

2 T. chili powder
1 T. paprika
1 T. garlic salt

1 T. pepper
1 t. cayenne pepper

Combine all seasonings in a small bowl.

A vintage-style oilcloth tablecloth with brightly colored fruit and flowers adds cheer to any dinner table. Its wipe-clean ease makes it practical for cookouts.

Tom's BBQ Ribs

Zesty Beef Fajitas

Zesty Beef Fajitas

Enjoy your favorite fajitas family-style at home...arrange all the fixin's on a big platter, pass the tortillas and let everyone make their own!

2 lbs. beef skirt steak
2 to 3 T. olive oil
1 green pepper, thinly sliced
1 red pepper, thinly sliced
1 onion, thinly sliced
1/2 lb. sliced mushrooms

4 to 6 8-inch flour tortillas, warmed
Garnish: sour cream, guacamole, shredded Monterey Jack cheese, shredded lettuce, chopped tomatoes

Place steak in a plastic zipping bag; set aside. Pour Fajita Marinade over steak; seal bag. Refrigerate for 6 to 8 hours, turning bag occasionally. Drain and discard marinade. Place steak on an oiled grill over medium-high heat. Grill to desired doneness, about 3 to 4 minutes per side; remove to a cutting board and cool slightly before slicing. Heat olive oil in a skillet over medium heat. Sauté vegetables until tender; drain. Fill warmed tortillas with sliced steak, vegetables and desired toppings. Makes 4 to 6 servings.

Fajita Marinade:

2 c. pineapple juice
1/4 c. lime juice
1 c. soy sauce

2 T. ground cumin
1-1/2 t. garlic, minced

Whisk together all ingredients in a bowl, making sure to break up any lumps. May be covered and refrigerated up to two days.

Heat tortillas right on the grill, turning when lightly browned. Wrap hot tortillas in a piece of aluminum foil to keep them warm.

Speedy Steak & Veggies

A summertime favorite...perfect for a rainy day when you've already promised a cookout for dinner.

juice of 1 lime
salt and pepper to taste
1-1/2 lbs. beef flank steak
1/2 bunch broccoli, cut into
  flowerets

2 c. baby carrots, sliced
2 ears sweet corn, husked and cut
  into 2-inch pieces
1 red onion, sliced into wedges
2 T. olive oil

Combine lime juice, salt and pepper; brush over both sides of beef. Place on a broiler pan and broil, 5 minutes per side, turning once. Set aside on a cutting board; keep warm. Toss vegetables with oil. Spoon onto a lightly greased baking sheet in a single layer. Bake at 475 degrees, turning once, for 10 to 15 minutes, until tender. Slice steak thinly on the diagonal and arrange on a platter, surrounded with vegetables. Serves 4 to 6.

Caramelized Onions

Great for topping hamburgers, steak, chicken or anything else off the grill. With a slow cooker, it's so easy.

8 onions, thickly sliced
1/4 c. butter, sliced
1/4 c. olive oil

1-1/2 t. sugar
salt to taste

Add all ingredients to a 5-quart slow cooker; stir to combine. Cook, uncovered, on low setting for 6 to 8 hours, stirring and scraping sides of crock often. Makes 12 servings.

Speedy Steak & Veggies

Susan's Slow-Cookin' Ribs

Juicy Steak & BBQ Pork

Susan's Slow-Cookin' Ribs

These ribs melt in your mouth! Enjoy with a side of sweet corn and potato salad, or shred and serve in sandwiches.

1 T. onion powder
1 t. red pepper flakes
1/2 t. dry mustard
1/2 t. garlic powder
1/2 t. allspice
1/2 t. cinnamon

3 lbs. boneless pork ribs, sliced
   into serving-size pieces
1 onion, sliced and divided
1/2 c. water
2 c. hickory-flavored barbecue
   sauce

Combine seasonings in a cup; mix well and rub over ribs. Arrange 1/3 of ribs in a 5-quart slow cooker. Top with 1/3 of onion slices. Repeat layering 2 more times, ending with onion. Pour water over all. Cover and cook on low setting for 8 to 10 hours. Drain and discard liquid from slow cooker. Pour barbecue sauce over ribs. Cover and cook on low setting for an additional one to 2 hours. Serves 6 to 8.

Ruby Sauce

Sweet, tart and absolutely the best sauce. Next time rhubarb is in season, try it on chicken, ribs or pulled pork.

1 c. brown sugar, packed
1 c. sugar
1 c. cider vinegar
1 t. ground ginger
1 t. cinnamon
1 t. allspice
1 t. paprika

1/2 t. ground cloves
1/2 t. red pepper flakes
1/2 t. salt
1/8 t. pepper
2 onions, finely chopped
4 c. rhubarb, finely chopped

Combine all ingredients except onions and rhubarb in a large saucepan over medium heat. Bring to a simmer; stir in onions and rhubarb. Cook for 45 minutes to one hour, until thickened and rhubarb is tender. Serve immediately, or cover and refrigerate. Serves 4 to 6.

Honey-Mustard Short Ribs

*All the flavor and fun of a Saturday night barbecue...
with none of the effort!*

3 to 4 lbs. bone-in beef short ribs
salt and pepper to taste
1 c. hickory smoke-flavored
   barbecue sauce
3 T. honey

1 T. Dijon mustard
3 cloves garlic, minced
2 T. cornstarch
2 T. cold water

Sprinkle ribs with salt and pepper; place in a 6-quart slow cooker and set aside. Combine barbecue sauce, honey, mustard, garlic and additional salt and pepper, if desired; spoon over ribs. Cover and cook on low setting for 6 to 7 hours, until tender. During the last 30 minutes of cooking, whisk cornstarch into water. Add to slow cooker, stirring until sauce is thickened. Serves 4.

82

Need a gift for your favorite backyard chef? Tuck a spatula, tongs and a basting brush inside an oven mitt. Add a jar of BBQ seasoning for a gift that's sure to be a hit.

Honey-Mustard Short Ribs

Chili Pepper Pork Satay

Chili Pepper Pork Satay

*Satay is small pieces of meat on skewers roasted on a grill. This recipe
from Indonesia is good with boneless chicken thighs too.*

20 shallots or 1 red onion, chopped
5 to 10 red chili peppers, to taste,
  or paprika
2-inch slice fresh ginger, peeled
  and chopped
1/2 to 1 T. lime juice
1 t. salt, or to taste

2 to 2-1/2 lbs. pork tenderloin, cut
  into 1-inch by 1/2-inch pieces
20 skewers
1 to 2 T. oil
cooked rice
Optional: thinly sliced cucumbers

In a blender, process shallots or onion, chili peppers or paprika, ginger,
lime juice and salt. Pour mixture over pork in a glass baking dish, stirring
to coat well. Cover and refrigerate pork for one to 2 hours. Drain, reserving
marinade. Arrange pork on skewers. Grill over a medium-hot charcoal fire
until pork is well done. Meanwhile, in a skillet over medium-high heat,
stir-fry reserved marinade in oil until vegetables are tender. To serve,
remove pork to a serving plate; spread with stir-fried mixture. Serve with
cooked rice; garnish with cucumbers, if desired. Makes 10 servings.

85

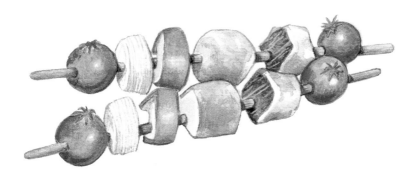

Make kabobs over a tabletop hibachi grill...cozy when it's
just dinner for two.

Summer Steak Skewers

These skewers go together quickly, grill up easily and are so flavorful.

1-1/2 lbs. beef sirloin steak, cut
   into 1-inch cubes
2 onions, cut into wedges

2 red, yellow and/or green peppers,
   cut into 1-inch squares
6 skewers

Place beef pieces in a large plastic zipping bag; pour in Honey Marinade. Seal bag and turn to coat. Refrigerate 8 hours to overnight, turning occasionally. Drain, discarding marinade. Thread beef and vegetables alternately onto skewers. Grill over medium heat for 12 to 14 minutes, or until beef reaches desired doneness, turning occasionally. Makes 6 servings.

Honey Marinade:

1/2 c. oil
1/4 c. soy sauce
3 T. honey

2 T. white vinegar
1/2 t. ground ginger
1 t. garlic powder

Combine all ingredients; mix well.

Soak wooden skewers in water for 30 minutes before adding meat and veggies. Skewers won't burn when grilled. Even easier...soak skewers, wrap and freeze. Ready whenever you are!

Summer Steak Skewers

For delectable kebabs and skewers, try full-flavored beef chuck roast, pork shoulder and chicken thighs. A little fat means it won't dry out quickly when grilled.

An instant-read digital thermometer is so handy for checking doneness...no guesswork needed. Insert thermometer in the thickest part of the meat. Recommended minimum temperatures:

- Beef = 145 degrees (medium rare)
- Burgers = 160 degrees
- Chicken = 165 degrees
- Fish & seafood = 145 degrees
- Pork = 145 degrees

Hickory, mesquite and apple wood chips add wonderful smoky flavor to grilled foods. Just soak in water, drain and scatter onto the hot grill or hot coals.

A great time-saver! If you have a favorite seasoning rub or mix that calls for lots of different herbs and spices, measure them out into several small plastic zipping bags and label. Later, when time is short, just pull out a bag.

Burgers, Dogs & More

Backyard Big
South-of-the-Border Burgers

One bite of this scrumptious, juicy burger, and you'll feel like a kid again, at the picnic table with family & friends.

4-oz. can chopped green chiles, drained
1/4 c. picante sauce
1/2 t. smoke-flavored cooking sauce
12 round buttery crackers, crushed
4-1/2 t. chili powder
1 T. ground cumin
1/2 t. salt

1/2 t. pepper
2 lbs. lean ground beef
1/2 lb. ground pork sausage
6 to 8 slices Pepper Jack cheese
6 to 8 sesame seed hamburger buns, split
Garnish: lettuce leaves, tomato slices

In a large bowl, combine chiles, sauces, cracker crumbs and seasonings; mix well. Crumble beef and sausage over mixture and mix well. Form into 6 to 8 patties. Grill, covered, over medium heat for 5 to 7 minutes on each side, until no longer pink. Top with cheese slices. Grill for one more minute, or until cheese is melted. Grill buns, cut-side down, for one to 2 minutes, until toasted. Serve burgers on buns, garnished as desired. Makes 6 to 8 servings.

Hamburger buns just taste better toasted! They won't get soggy either. Lightly butter buns and place on a hot grill for 30 seconds to one minute, or until toasted to taste, turning once.

Backyard Big South-of-the-Border Burgers

Beverly's Bacon Burgers

Beverly's Bacon Burgers

A great way to get some extra veggies into your kids' meals!

1-1/2 lbs. ground beef
1 baking potato, peeled and diced
2 carrots, peeled and grated
1/2 onion, grated
1 egg, beaten
1 t. dried parsley

3/4 t. garlic, minced
1/2 t. salt
pepper to taste
6 to 7 slices bacon
6 to 7 sandwich buns, split

In a large bowl, combine all ingredients except bacon and buns. Mix well; form into 6 to 7 patties. Wrap a bacon slice around each patty and secure with a wooden toothpick. Grill over medium heat to desired doneness. Serve on buns. Makes 6 to 7 servings.

Weekend Treat Burgers

Hearty appetites love these big half-pound burgers, but you could make 6 smaller burgers if your family's appetites are lighter. Top with sautéed mushrooms for an extra special meal.

2/3 c. shredded provolone cheese
1/2 c. green pepper, diced
1/2 c. onion, chopped

salt and pepper to taste
2 lbs. ground beef chuck
4 sesame seed kaiser rolls, split

Toss together cheese, green pepper, onion, salt and pepper in a large bowl. Add beef; mix well and form into 4 burgers. Grill or pan-fry over medium-high heat for 4 to 5 minutes on each side. Serve on rolls. Serves 4.

Tina's All-Star Sliders on Cornbread Buns

Flavorful little burgers on homemade buns...what a treat!

3/4 lb. ground beef chuck	1 t. garlic powder
1 egg, lightly beaten	1/4 t. chili powder
1/3 c. onion, chopped	1/4 t. salt
1/3 c. shredded Pepper Jack cheese	hot pepper sauce to taste

Make Cornbread Buns; set aside to cool. In a large bowl, combine all ingredients; mix well. Form into twelve 2-1/2 inch patties. Grill over medium-high heat for 3 to 4 minutes per side. Serve sliders on split buns. Makes 6 servings, 2 buns each.

Cornbread Buns:

3/4 c. yellow cornmeal	1/2 t. pepper
3/4 c. all-purpose flour	3/4 c. sour cream
1 T. sugar	2 T. oil
2 t. baking powder	2 eggs, lightly beaten
3/4 t. salt	

Combine dry ingredients in a bowl; mix well. Add remaining ingredients; stir just until smooth. Spray 12 muffin cups with non-stick vegetable spray. Fill muffin cups 3/4 full, spreading batter to edges. Bake at 350 degrees for 8 to 10 minutes, until centers spring back when touched. Cool buns in tin for about 5 minutes; remove to a wire rack.

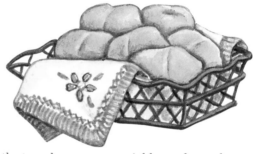

For burgers that cook up more quickly and evenly, press your thumb into the center of each patty to make an indentation.

Tina's All-Star Sliders on Cornbread Buns

State Fair Italian Sausages

Burgers, Dogs & More

State Fair Italian Sausages

If you love the Italian sausages sold at the fair, but don't care for grilled onions and peppers, try this! The contrast of the hot spicy sausages with the cold crisp lettuce is delicious.

6 to 8 Italian pork sausage links
1/2 head lettuce, thinly sliced or
   shredded

zesty Italian salad dressing to taste
6 to 8 hot dog buns, split
Garnish: mustard

In a large saucepan, cover sausages with water. Bring to a boil over high heat; boil for 10 to 15 minutes. Drain sausages well; grill over medium heat until browned. While sausages are grilling, place lettuce in a bowl; add just enough dressing to coat lettuce well. To serve, place sausages on buns; garnish with mustard and top with lettuce mixture. Makes 6 to 8 servings.

97

Need a super-quick marinade? Grab a bottle of Italian salad dressing... it's terrific with just about any kind of meat. Add 1/4 to 1/2 cup marinade per one to 2 pounds of meat. You only need enough to coat, not cover!

Santa Fe Grilled Veggie Pizzas

Serve these fresh and delicious pizzas for a meatless dinner, or cut into small squares and serve as appetizers.

10-oz. tube refrigerated pizza
    dough
1 lb. portabella mushrooms, stems
    removed
1 red pepper, quartered
1 yellow pepper, quartered
1 zucchini, cut lengthwise into
    1/2-inch thick slices

1 yellow squash, cut lengthwise
    into 1/2-inch thick slices
3/4 t. salt
1 c. Alfredo sauce
1-1/4 c. smoked mozzarella
    cheese, shredded

Lightly dust 2 baking sheets with flour; set aside. On a lightly floured surface, press dough into a 15-inch x 11-inch rectangle. Cut into quarters; place 2 on each baking sheet and set aside. Lightly coat vegetables with non-stick vegetable spray; season with salt. Grill vegetables over medium-high heat until tender, about 10 minutes. Slice mushrooms and peppers; cut squash in half crosswise and set aside. Grill pizza dough, 2 pieces at a time, for one minute, or until golden. With tongs, turn dough over and grill 30 more seconds, or until firm. Return to baking sheets. Spread sauce over crusts; top with vegetables and cheese. Grill pizzas, covered, for 2 to 3 minutes, until cheese melts. Makes 4 servings.

Stem and seed a sweet pepper in a flash...hold the pepper upright on a cutting board. Use a sharp knife to slice each of the sides from the pepper. You'll then have 4 large seedless pieces ready for chopping.

Santa Fe Grilled Veggie Pizzas

Incredible Mini Burger Bites

Incredible Mini Burger Bites

Tasty little sliders for for football parties and get-togethers.
They're oven-baked all at once...so easy!

2 lbs. lean ground beef
1-1/2 oz. pkg. onion soup mix
2 eggs, beaten
1/2 c. dry bread crumbs
3 T. water
1/2 t. garlic salt

1 t. pepper
24 dinner rolls or slider buns, split
6 slices American cheese, quartered
Garnish: catsup, mustard, shredded
    lettuce, thinly sliced onion, dill
    pickles

In a large bowl, combine all ingredients except rolls, cheese and garnish.
Mix well; cover and refrigerate for one hour. Spread beef mixture over a
greased large baking sheet. Cover with plastic wrap and roll out evenly with
a rolling pin. Discard plastic wrap; bake at 400 degrees for 12 minutes, or
until no longer pink in the center. Slice into 24 squares with a pizza cutter.
Top each roll with a burger square, a cheese slice and desired garnishes.
Makes 2 dozen sliders.

101

If you are ever at a loss to support a flagging conversation,
introduce the subject of eating.
-Leigh Hunt

Sizzling Herb Burgers

When your backyard grill is surrounded by fresh garden herbs, what do you do? Make herb burgers, of course!

3 lbs. ground beef
1 c. Italian-flavored dry bread
  crumbs
3 eggs, beaten
3 cloves garlic, minced
2 T. fresh garlic chives, chopped

2 T. fresh basil, chopped
2 T. fresh flat-leaf parsley, chopped
1 t. fresh rosemary, chopped
salt and pepper to taste
8 to 10 hamburger buns, split

In a large bowl, mix together all ingredients except buns. Form into 8 to 10 patties. Grill burgers over medium-high heat to desired doneness, about 5 to 7 minutes on each side. Serve burgers on buns. Makes 8 to 10 servings.

Cindy's Special Sauce

This sauce is so good on charcoal grilled burgers, hot dogs, fries and more! You'll find yourself using it all summer long.

1/4 c. butter
1 onion, chopped
24-oz. bottle catsup

1/2 c. white vinegar
3/4 c. brown sugar, packed

Melt butter in a saucepan over medium heat. Add onion and cook until onion is tender, about 5 minutes. Add remaining ingredients; simmer for 5 minutes. Use immediately, or cover and refrigerate. Makes 4 cups.

Sizzling Herb Burgers

Grilled Portabella Burgers

Grilled Portabella Burgers

So flavorful that you'll never miss the meat!

1/4 c. butter, melted
2 T. fresh basil, chopped
2 T. balsamic vinegar
4 t. garlic, minced
4 large portabella mushroom caps
4 slices sweet onion

4 whole-wheat hamburger buns,
  split
4 slices Muenster cheese
Garnish: romaine lettuce, tomato
  slices

Combine butter, basil, vinegar and garlic in a small bowl. Brush butter mixture lightly over mushroom caps and onion slices. Grill mushrooms and onion over medium heat for 4 to 5 minutes per side, turning once and brushing with remaining butter mixture. Brush any remaining butter mixture over cut sides of buns. Toast buns cut-side down on the grill for one to 2 minutes. Place each mushroom cap in a bun; top with a cheese slice, lettuce and tomato. Makes 4 servings.

Spectacular Sh'rooms

A delectable side for a fantastic steak dinner! For the best results, choose small or medium-size mushrooms.

1 lb. whole mushrooms, stems
  trimmed
1/4 c. canola oil
1/4 c. water

1-oz. pkg. ranch salad dressing
  mix
1 T. balsamic vinegar
1/8 t. pepper

Place mushrooms in a one-gallon plastic zipping bag. In a small bowl, combine remaining ingredients. Blend well and pour over mushrooms; seal bag and shake to coat. Refrigerate for 30 minutes, turning occasionally. Drain; arrange mushrooms on a broiler pan. Broil for 8 to 10 minutes, until tender and golden. Serves 4 to 6.

Mom's Eggplant Sandwich

*Packed with eggplant and squash, this sandwich will let the veggie eaters
at your next cookout know that you haven't forgotten about them.
You may even choose this over a hamburger yourself!*

1 eggplant, sliced 1/2-inch thick
2 zucchini or yellow squash, sliced
   1/2-inch thick
2 T. olive oil
salt and pepper to taste
3 to 4 T. mayonnaise

1 French baguette loaf, halved
   lengthwise
1 to 2 tomatoes, thinly sliced
1/4 c. grated Parmesan cheese,
   divided

Drizzle eggplant and squash slices with olive oil. Season with salt and
pepper; arrange in a wire grill basket. Grill over medium heat until
vegetables are tender and golden; remove from grill. Spread mayonnaise
over cut sides of loaf. Arrange tomato slices on bottom half of loaf; sprinkle
with salt, pepper and half of Parmesan cheese. Layer grilled vegetables over
tomatoes. Sprinkle with remaining cheese; add top half and slice into
quarters. Makes 4 servings.

106

Remember the vegetarians at your next cookout. Pita rounds stuffed
with grilled veggies are a delicious choice.

Mom's Eggplant Sandwich

Key West Burgers

Key West Burgers

For a real Key West experience, enjoy these flavorful burgers with a frozen tropical drink.

1 lb. ground beef
3 T. Key lime juice
1/4 c. fresh cilantro, chopped
salt and pepper to taste

4 hamburger buns, split and
toasted
Garnish: lettuce leaves

In a bowl, combine beef, lime juice, cilantro, salt and pepper. Form beef mixture into 4 patties. Spray a large skillet with non-stick vegetable spray. Cook patties over medium heat for 6 minutes. Flip patties, cover skillet and cook for another 6 minutes. Place lettuce on bottom halves of buns and top with patties. Add Creamy Burger Spread onto bun tops and close sandwiches. Serves 4.

Creamy Burger Spread:

8-oz. pkg. cream cheese, softened
8-oz. container sour cream

3 green onion tops, chopped

Combine all ingredients; stir until completely blended. Cover and refrigerate at least 15 minutes.

Delicious burgers begin with ground beef chuck labeled as 80/20. A little fat in the beef adds flavor...there's no need to purchase expensive ground sirloin.

Grilled Cuban Sandwiches

A great combination of flavors! Grill sandwiches on an outdoor grill or on a panini press, if you prefer.

4 submarine rolls, split
mustard to taste
1/3 lb. deli roast pork, thinly sliced
8 slices Swiss cheese

1/3 lb. deli baked ham, thinly
  sliced
dill pickle sandwich slices to taste
1 T. butter, softened

Spread cut sides of rolls with mustard. Layer bottom halves of rolls with pork, cheese, ham and pickles. Add top halves; spread butter lightly over outside of rolls. Gently flatten sandwiches with your hand; wrap individually in aluminum foil. Grill sandwiches over medium heat until heated through and cheese is melted. Unwrap sandwiches; return to grill and toast lightly on both sides. Makes 4 servings.

Savory Steak Sliders

These delectable little sandwiches are sure to be a hit at your next party! Perfect for a casual Christmas dinner too.

1/2 c. balsamic vinegar
3 T. Worcestershire sauce
1 clove garlic, minced
1-1/2 lbs. beef top round steak

16 slider buns, split and warmed
Garnish: horseradish sauce, Dijon
  mustard

In a large plastic zipping bag, combine vinegar, Worcestershire sauce and garlic; squeeze bag to mix. Add steak to bag; turn to coat well. Seal bag and refrigerate for 4 to 6 hours, turning several times to coat steak. Preheat broiler to high. Remove steak from bag; discard marinade. Place steak on a lightly greased broiler pan; place pan 2 to 3 inches under broiler. Broil for 6 to 8 minutes on each side, until medium-rare. Remove from oven; let stand for 5 minutes. Thinly slice steak on the diagonal. Divide steak slices among bun bottoms; garnish as desired and add tops of buns. Makes 16 sliders.

Grilled Cuban Sandwiches

Jax's Cheeseburger Pizza

Jax's Cheeseburger Pizza

Need something fast and easy for a crowd? This is sure to please!

1 lb. ground turkey
1/2 c. onion, diced
1/2 t. garlic salt
1/2 t. pepper
2 12-inch prebaked Italian
  pizza crusts

catsup and mustard to taste
16-oz. jar sliced bread & butter
  pickles, drained
8-oz. pkg. shredded Cheddar
  cheese

In a skillet over medium heat, brown turkey and onion; sprinkle with garlic salt and pepper. Drain and set aside. Place pizza crusts on ungreased baking sheets. Swirl catsup onto crusts, as you would do on a hamburger bun. Swirl mustard over the catsup (no need to smooth out or mix together). Divide turkey mixture evenly between the 2 crusts; arrange pickles on top of turkey. Sprinkle evenly with cheese. Bake at 425 degrees for 12 to 15 minutes, until cheese has melted. Cut into wedges to serve. Makes 2 pizzas, 8 servings each.

113

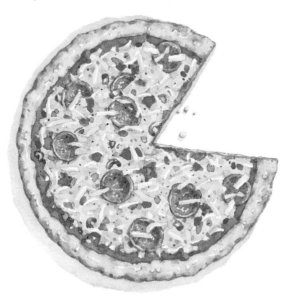

Are the kids having friends over for dinner? Bright-colored plastic flying disks make great no-spill holders for flimsy paper plates.

Grilled Sicilian-Style Pizza

Pizza hot off the grill...delicious! Feel free to add some thinly sliced pepperoni, if you like.

14-oz. prebaked Italian pizza crust
2 roma tomatoes, thinly sliced
1 yellow or red tomato, thinly sliced
1/4 lb. fresh mozzarella cheese, thinly sliced
1/3 c. Kalamata olives, halved
1 T. olive oil
1 c. fresh escarole or curly endive, coarsely chopped
1/4 c. shredded Parmesan cheese
pepper to taste

Fold a 24-inch by 18-inch piece of heavy-duty aluminum foil in half lengthwise. Place pizza crust on foil; turn edges of foil up to edge of pizza. Arrange tomato and cheese slices over crust; top with olives. Drizzle oil over all. In a grill with a cover, arrange hot coals around a drip pan for indirect grilling. Test for medium heat above pan. Place pizza on grill rack. Cover and grill over medium heat for about 6 minutes, until pizza is nearly heated through. Top with escarole or endive; grill another 2 minutes. Remove from grill; sprinkle with Parmesan cheese and pepper. Cut into wedges. Makes 4 to 6 servings.

Breakfast pizza on the grill! Brush a prebaked pizza crust with olive oil and grill on one side until toasty. Turn over and top with lightly scrambled eggs, crispy bacon and a handful of cheese. Cover and cook for a few more minutes, until cheese is melted.

Grilled Sicilian-Style Pizza

Grilled Dogs & Kraut

Grilled Dogs & Kraut

Turn 'em into Reuben dogs...top with shredded Swiss cheese.

3 slices bacon, crisply cooked and crumbled
1/2 to 3/4 c. Thousand Island salad dressing
3/4 c. sauerkraut, well drained
8 hot dogs
8 hot dog buns, split and toasted

Combine bacon, salad dressing and sauerkraut in a bowl; set aside. Grill hot dogs to desired doneness. Place hot dogs in buns; top with spoonfuls of bacon mixture. Makes 8 servings.

Hank's Hot Sauce

An old favorite! This sauce has a nice flavor for hot dogs and hamburgers, and isn't extremely spicy.

1 lb. ground beef
1 T. Worcestershire sauce
1 T. chili powder
1 T. paprika
1 T. allspice
1/2 T. cayenne pepper
1 t. garlic salt
1 t. onion salt

Place beef in a medium saucepan; add enough water to cover beef. Add remaining ingredients; bring to a boil over medium heat. Reduce heat; simmer for about one hour, stirring occasionally to break up beef. Serve immediately, or keep refrigerated and rewarm at serving time. Makes 3 cups; serves 12 to 15.

Even an old boot tastes good if it is cooked over charcoal.
-Italian Proverb

Red Devil Franks

Looking for a good rainy-day recipe when you can't grill outdoors? The homemade sauce on these hot dogs can't be beat...it has such a delicious and unique flavor!

2 to 4 T. butter
1 c. onion, finely chopped
2 cloves garlic, chopped
1-1/2 T. Worcestershire sauce
1-1/2 T. mustard
1-1/2 t. sugar

1/2 t. salt
1/8 t. pepper
1/2 c. chili sauce
8 hot dogs
8 hot dog buns, split

Melt butter in a skillet over medium heat. Cook onion and garlic in butter until translucent. Stir in remaining ingredients except hot dogs and buns. Cook, stirring occasionally, until heated through, about 5 minutes. Split hot dogs lengthwise and arrange in a single layer in a broiler pan. Spoon some of the sauce over hot dogs; broil until bubbly, about 5 minutes. Serve hot dogs on buns, topped with any remaining sauce. Makes 8 servings.

A fun and simple meal...try a chili dog bar! Along with grilled hot dogs and buns, set out chili, shredded cheese, sauerkraut, chopped onions and your favorite condiments.

Red Devil Franks

Colossal Hero Sandwich

Colossal Hero Sandwich

A classic for your picnic basket!

1 loaf Italian bread
2 c. romaine lettuce, shredded
2 T. Italian salad dressing
1/4 t. dried oregano
1/2 lb. sliced deli salami
6-oz. pkg. sliced provolone cheese
1 to 2 tomatoes, thinly sliced

1/2 lb. sliced deli ham
7-oz. jar roasted red peppers,
   drained and patted dry
6 pepperoncini, sliced
2-1/4 oz. can sliced black olives,
   drained
1 red onion, thinly sliced

Slice loaf in half lengthwise. With a fork, carefully hollow out the center of bottom half of loaf; reserved pulled-out bread for another use. Fill hollow with lettuce. Combine dressing and oregano in a small bowl; mix well and drizzle over lettuce. Layer remaining ingredients over lettuce. Cover with top of loaf and slice into individual portions. Serves 6 to 8.

121

To make cutting easy, just push long toothpicks into the sandwich, then cut between the toothpicks with a serrated knife.

Turkey Gobbler Sandwich

A quick turkey & veggie sandwich that you're sure to love! Just add chips and a tossed salad for an easy weeknight meal.

1 loaf French bread
1 c. basil pesto sauce
8 slices provolone cheese, divided
8 to 10 slices deli turkey breast

2 zucchini, thinly sliced lengthwise
1 tomato, thinly sliced
pepper to taste

Slice top 1/4 off loaf and set aside; hollow out bottom of loaf. Spread pesto over insides of both parts of loaf. Layer 4 cheese slices and all of turkey, zucchini and tomato in bottom of loaf; sprinkle with pepper to taste. Arrange remaining cheese slices; replace top of loaf. Wrap loaf completely in aluminum foil. Grill over medium heat for 20 to 30 minutes, until sandwich is heated through and cheese is melted. Unwrap carefully; cut into thick slices. Makes 4 to 6 servings.

Whip up a tasty dipping sauce for French fries...half mayonnaise, half Dijon mustard and a shake of cayenne pepper for spice.

Turkey Gobbler Sandwich

Chicken-Apple Sliders

Chicken-Apple Sliders

Slider sandwiches are just the right size, especially when paired with salads and sides. This is one of our favorites.

1 Granny Smith apple, cored
   and shredded
1/4 c. celery, finely chopped
1/2 t. poultry seasoning
1/4 t. pepper
1/4 t. salt
2 T. honey
1 lb. ground chicken

8 slices bacon, crisply cooked,
   crumbled and divided
Optional: 2 slices favorite cheese,
   quartered
8 slider sandwich rolls, split and
   toasted
Garnish: mayonnaise, shredded
   lettuce, sliced tomato and onion

In a large bowl, combine apple, celery and seasonings; toss to mix. Add honey, chicken and half of bacon. Stir until combined; do not overmix. Form into 8 small patties. Grill patties over medium heat for about 4 minutes per side, until chicken is no longer pink. If desired, top each patty with a piece of cheese during the last few minutes of cooking. Place patties on rolls; top with remaining bacon and other toppings, as desired. Makes 4 servings, 2 sliders each.

125

BBQ Chicken Melts

A tasty, quick dinner to fix on the grill...why eat fast-food chicken sandwiches?

4 boneless, skinless chicken
   breasts
1/2 c. barbecue sauce, divided
4 slices deli ham

4 slices provolone cheese
4 hamburger buns, split
Optional: mayonnaise to taste

Brush chicken breasts with half of the barbecue sauce. Grill over medium heat on both sides, until golden and chicken juices run clear. Brush chicken with remaining barbecue sauce. Top each piece with a slice of ham and a slice of cheese. Grill just until cheese is melted. Serve chicken on buns with a little mayonnaise, if desired. Makes 4 servings.

Pepperoni Pizza Burgers

If your family just loves pizza and burgers, this recipe will make for a great change at mealtime.

1-1/2 lbs. lean ground beef
1/2 lb. Italian ground pork sausage
1/2 t. Italian seasoning
12 slices mozzarella and/or
    provolone cheese

3-oz. pkg. sliced pepperoni
6 kaiser rolls, split
softened butter to taste
3/4 c. pizza sauce
grated Parmesan cheese to taste

In a large bowl, combine beef, sausage and seasoning. Mix well; form into 6 patties. Grill patties over medium heat to desired doneness, 3 to 4 minutes per side. When patties are nearly done, top each patty with 2 slices cheese and 5 to 6 slices pepperoni. Cover grill; continue cooking just until pepperoni is warmed through and cheese is melted. Spread cut sides of rolls with softened butter. Toast rolls on the grill until crisp and golden. Spread cut sides of rolls with sauce; sprinkle with Parmesan cheese. Serve burgers on buns. Makes 6 servings.

It's a snap to clean the grate after cooking. A little water and a scouring pad or grill brush will do the trick, or wad up a ball of aluminum foil. Rinse the grate well and dry before storing.

Pepperoni Pizza Burgers

To form hamburger patties in a flash, shape ground beef into a log and partially freeze it. Cut the log into slices, lay on a baking sheet and freeze until solid. Remove patties to freezer bags...perfect hamburgers when you're ready for them. Just the thing for that 5-pound family pack of beef!

When burgers or hot dogs are on the menu, set up a topping bar with catsup, mustard, pickle relish, chili sauce and shredded cheese. Everyone can just help themselves to their favorites.

Microwave raw onions on high in a covered container for one to 2 minutes before using. They'll be easier to peel and will also lose some of the "hot" taste. Helpful to know if you're serving them uncooked on hamburgers or in salads.

Turn those leftover buns into garlic bread in a jiffy! Spread with softened butter, sprinkle with garlic salt and broil until toasty.

Classic Cookout Sides

Tomato Salad With Grilled Bread

Chock-full of sun-ripe tomatoes and juicy watermelon, this variation on Italian panzanella salad is sure to please.

3 lbs. ripe tomatoes, cut into chunks
1 cucumber, peeled and sliced
4-oz. container crumbled feta cheese
1/4 c. balsamic vinegar
1/4 t. salt
1/4 t. pepper
8 thick slices crusty Italian bread

6 T. olive oil, divided
2 c. watermelon, cut into 1/2-inch cubes
1 red onion, very thinly sliced and separated into rings
3.8-oz. can sliced black olives, drained
1/2 c. fresh basil, torn

In a large serving bowl, combine tomatoes, cucumber, cheese, vinegar, salt and pepper. Toss to mix; cover and chill for one hour. Shortly before serving time, brush both sides of bread with 2 tablespoons olive oil. Place bread on a hot grill; grill on both sides until toasted and grill marks form. Cut bread into large cubes. Add bread cubes, remaining oil and other ingredients to chilled tomato mixture. Toss very lightly and serve. Makes 6 servings.

Invite friends and neighbors to a good old-fashioned block party. Set up picnic tables, arrange lots of chairs in the shade and invite everyone to bring a favorite dish. You'll make some wonderful memories together!

Tomato Salad With Grilled Bread

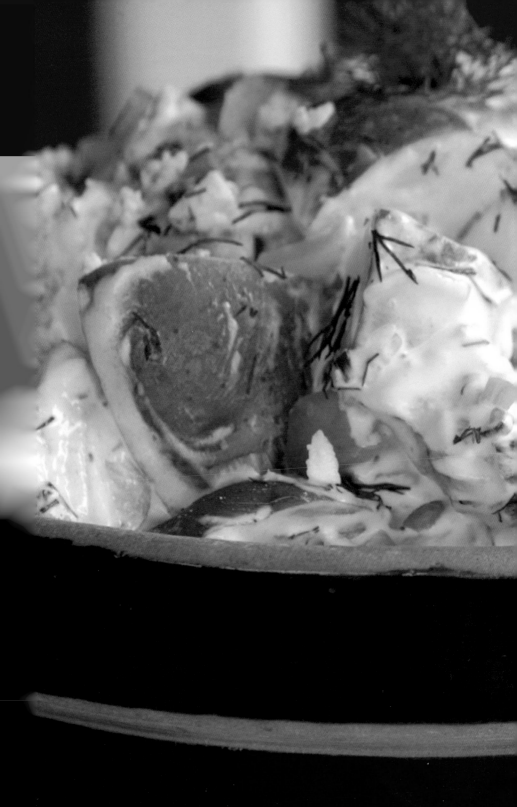

Dilly Blue Cheese Potato Salad

Dilly Blue Cheese Potato Salad

Try this wonderful new spin on potato salad...redskin potatoes combined with tangy blue cheese and sour cream.

1 c. mayonnaise
1 c. sour cream
2 t. lemon juice
1 bunch green onions, chopped
5 stalks celery, chopped
1/2 c. fresh dill, chopped

1/2 c. crumbled blue cheese
3 lbs. new redskin potatoes,
    quartered and cooked
1 t. salt
pepper to taste

Blend together mayonnaise, sour cream and lemon juice in a large bowl. Add onions, celery and dill; fold in blue cheese and potatoes. Add salt and pepper to taste. Cover and chill overnight. Makes 10 servings.

Mother's Cucumber Salad

Cool, crisp and delicious, this simple salad tastes even better the longer it marinates in the refrigerator.

3 to 4 cucumbers, peeled and
   thinly sliced
3 T. salt
1/4 c. cider vinegar
2 t. sugar

1/2 t. onion powder
1/4 t. celery seed
1/4 t. pepper
Optional: 1/2 c. sliced red onion

Place cucumbers in a large bowl; add salt and enough water to cover. Cover and shake to mix salt. Refrigerate several hours to overnight. Drain cucumbers, but do not rinse; return to bowl. Stir together vinegar, sugar and seasonings; mix well and pour over cucumbers. Add onion, if desired. Cover and shake gently to mix. Refrigerate until serving time. Serves 6.

Keep salads chilled...nestle the serving bowl into a larger bowl filled with crushed ice.

Greek Pasta Salad

*Penne, rotini and bowtie pasta work equally well in this classic recipe...
pick your favorite!*

3 c. cooked elbow macaroni
3 c. sliced mushrooms, diced
15 cherry tomatoes, halved
1 c. yellow or red pepper, sliced

1/2 c. green onion, chopped
3/4 c. sliced black olives, drained
1 c. crumbled feta cheese
Optional: 3/4 c. pepperoni, diced

Combine all ingredients in a large bowl. Pour Oil & Vinegar Dressing over top; toss until evenly coated. Cover and chill 2 hours to overnight. Makes 10 to 12 servings.

Oil & Vinegar Dressing:

1/2 c. olive oil
1/2 c. red wine vinegar
1-1/2 t. garlic powder
1-1/2 t. dried basil

1-1/2 t. dried oregano
3/4 t. pepper
3/4 t. sugar

Whisk together ingredients in a small bowl.

String white twinkly lights in the trees and bushes around your patio
for an enchanting twilight atmosphere.

Greek Pasta Salad

Zesty Marinated Garden Veggies

Classic Cookout Sides

Zesty Marinated Garden Veggies

A great way to enjoy fresh-picked vegetables, whether from your own garden or from your favorite farmers' market. An easy make-ahead.

1 c. cucumber, sliced
1 c. yellow squash, sliced
1 c. zucchini, sliced
1 c. tomato, quartered
1/2 c. broccoli flowerets
1/2 c. cauliflower flowerets
1/2 c. red onion, sliced
1/2 c. green pepper, sliced
1/2 c. celery, sliced
8-oz. bottle zesty Italian dressing
1 t. salt-free herb seasoning

Combine all vegetables in a large bowl. Add salad dressing and seasoning; toss to mix. Cover and refrigerate for 2 hours before serving. Makes 10 to 12 servings.

Sweet-as-Sugar Snap Peas

The sweetness of the snap peas is perfect with just a touch of tanginess from the red onion...delicious!

1 lb. sugar snap peas
1/2 c. red onion, thinly sliced
2 cloves garlic, minced
2 T. olive oil
1/2 t. salt
1/4 t. pepper

Cover peas with water in a large saucepan and boil for 3 minutes; drain and rinse with cold water. Combine all ingredients; toss to coat. Cover and chill for one hour to overnight. Serves 4.

Classic Cookout Sides

Raspberry Spinach Salad

Everyone loves this salad. Excellent for picnics...
just toss it when you get there!

6-oz. pkg. baby spinach
1 pt. raspberries
1 c. pecan pieces
1/4 c. red onion, finely chopped

2 kiwis, peeled and cubed
1/2 c. raspberry vinaigrette salad
  dressing

In a large bowl, toss together all ingredients. Serve immediately. Serves 4.

He who shares the joy in what he's grown,
Spreads joy abroad and doubles his own.
-Anonymous

Raspberry Spinach Salad

Country Potato Bake

Country Potato Bake

Made with frozen hashbrowns, this scrumptious side is oven-ready in a jiffy.

20-oz. pkg. frozen shredded
  hashbrowns, thawed
10-3/4 oz. can cream of
  chicken soup
1 c. sour cream

1/4 c. butter, melted
1 c. shredded Cheddar cheese
6 slices bacon, crisply cooked and
  chopped
2.8-oz. can French fried onions

Spread hashbrowns evenly in a greased 13"x9" baking pan; set aside.
Mix soup, sour cream and butter together; spread over hashbrowns.
Sprinkle with cheese, bacon and onions. Bake, covered, at 350 degrees
for 45 minutes, or until bubbly and golden. Makes 10 servings.

Packing for a campfire cookout? Save time by chopping veggies at
home and placing them in small bags for the cooler. Or choose a recipe
using mostly canned ingredients...don't forget the can opener!

Classic Cookout Sides

Grilled Bacon Corn on the Cob

The bacon flavors the corn...delicious!

6 ears sweet corn, husked
1/4 c. butter, softened

salt and pepper to taste
6 slices bacon

Coat each ear of corn with 2 teaspoons butter; season with salt and pepper. Wrap a slice of bacon around each ear. Wrap each ear loosely in heavy-duty aluminum foil. Place corn on a grill over medium heat. Cook for about 30 minutes, turning frequently, until bacon is crisp. Unwrap carefully to serve. Makes 6 servings.

Smoky Grilled Corn

Jazz up some sweet corn! You'll find smoked paprika in the grocery's spice aisle.

8 ears sweet corn, husked
4 T. olive oil, divided
1 T. kosher salt, divided

1 T. pepper, divided
1 T. smoked paprika, divided

Divide corn between 2 large plastic zipping bags. To each bag, add 2 tablespoons oil, 1/2 tablespoon salt, 1/2 tablespoon pepper and 1/2 tablespoon paprika. Close bags and gently toss to coat corn. Remove corn from bags; arrange on a grill over medium-high heat. Grill, turning often, until lightly golden, about 25 minutes. Makes 8 servings.

142

Grilled Bacon Corn on the Cob

Grilled Potato Pouches

Classic Cookout Sides

Grilled Potato Pouches

Try both redskin and Yukon gold potatoes in this fun and easy recipe.

5 potatoes, peeled and sliced
1 onion, thinly sliced
6 T. butter, sliced
1 c. shredded Cheddar cheese
2 T. dried parsley

2 T. Worcestershire sauce
1/2 t. salt
1/4 t. pepper
1/3 c. chicken broth

Place potatoes and onion on a 22-inch piece of heavy-duty aluminum foil. Dot with butter. Sprinkle with cheese, parsley, sauce, salt and pepper. Fold up around potatoes; drizzle with broth. Seal well. Place on a hot grill for 35 minutes, or until potatoes are tender. Serves 6.

Savory Stuffed Potatoes

A fabulous side for grilled steaks and chops. If you like, oven-bake the potatoes ahead of time, then cut, fill and grill until heated through.

6 baking potatoes
1 red onion, sliced
6 slices bacon, crisply cooked and
  crumbled
6 to 7 mushrooms, sliced

1/2 c. butter, thinly sliced
garlic powder, salt and pepper to
  taste
1 c. green onions, chopped
Garnish: fresh parsley sprigs

Cut 4 to 5 slits across each potato without cutting through. Fill the slits evenly with red onion, bacon, mushrooms and butter slices. Sprinkle with seasonings; top with green onion. Wrap each potato with aluminum foil; seal tightly. Grill, covered, over medium-high heat for 35 to 45 minutes, until potatoes are tender. Garnish with parsley at serving time. Serves 6.

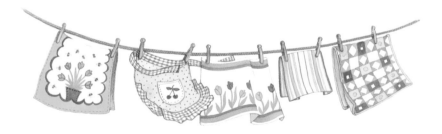

Cajun Oven Fries

Why settle for ordinary fries? These tender potatoes are hot and spicy.

3 to 4 T. olive oil
2 T. hot pepper sauce
1 t. dried thyme
1 t. ground cumin

1 t. paprika
4 potatoes, cut into wedges
salt and pepper to taste

Combine oil, hot sauce and seasonings in a large bowl; toss with potatoes. Arrange potatoes in a single layer on an ungreased non-stick baking sheet. Sprinkle with salt and pepper. Bake at 450 degrees for 20 minutes, turning once, until tender. Serves 4.

Sun-warmed ripe tomatoes from the farmers' market...is there anything more irresistible? Serve them simply, drizzled with a little Italian salad dressing and some chopped fresh basil.

Cajun Oven Fries

Tangy Summer Slaw

Tangy Summer Slaw

This coleslaw is colorful and loaded with fresh flavors...it's a must-try!

1 head red cabbage, shredded
1 head green cabbage, shredded
1 carrot, peeled and shredded
1 onion, finely chopped
1 green pepper, finely chopped
16-oz. bottle red wine vinegar &
   oil salad dressing

1/4 c. olive oil
1/4 c. sugar
1 T. Dijon mustard
1 t. caraway seed
salt and pepper to taste

Toss together all vegetables in a large salad bowl; set aside. In a separate bowl, combine remaining ingredients; pour over vegetables. Cover and refrigerate until ready to serve. Toss at serving time. Serves 8 to 10.

149

Grill up a salad! Choose small heads of romaine; don't separate the leaves. Rinse, pat dry and spritz with olive oil. Grill over high heat for 2 to 3 minutes per side, until lightly wilted and golden. Serve lettuce drizzled with balsamic vinaigrette, or chop and use in a Caesar salad.

Hot & Sweet Coleslaw

*If you prefer slaw without a lot of mayonnaise, you'll like this one.
Great with pulled pork sandwiches.*

8 c. green cabbage, shredded
1 c. red cabbage, shredded
4 carrots, peeled and shredded
1 yellow onion, grated
1/2 c. mayonnaise
2 T. mustard

2 t. cider vinegar
1/4 c. sugar
1 t. pepper
1/4 t. cayenne pepper
Optional: salt and additional pepper
    to taste

In a large bowl, toss together vegetables. In a separate bowl, whisk together mayonnaise, mustard, vinegar, sugar and peppers. Toss mayonnaise mixture with cabbage mixture; season with salt and additional pepper, if desired. Cover and refrigerate overnight before serving. Makes 10 to 12 servings.

Add extra texture to fresh veggies for salads and relish plates. Use a crinkle cutter or a spiral slicer to cut them into slices and sticks.

Hot & Sweet Coleslaw

Beans & Weenies

Classic Cookout Sides

Beans & Weenies

A year 'round favorite... a slow-cooker standby for summer picnics, yet hearty and satisfying during cold weather too.

1 lb. hot dogs, sliced into bite-size
    pieces
3 16-oz. cans pork & beans
1/4 c. onion, chopped

1/2 c. catsup
1/4 c. molasses
2 t. mustard

Combine all ingredients in a 4-quart slow cooker; stir well. Cover and cook on low setting for 3 to 4 hours. Makes 8 servings.

Grilled Fresh Veggie Combo

Great for your next trip to the farmers' market. Feel free to add any favorites like green and yellow beans, sugar snap peas and green peppers.

1 zucchini, thinly sliced
1 yellow squash, thinly sliced
1 red onion, thinly sliced
1 T. garlic, minced

olive oil to taste
fresh basil, oregano, rosemary or
    parsley to taste, chopped

Use a vegetable grill basket or a piece of heavy-duty aluminum foil with the sides rolled up to form a bowl. Coat with non-stick vegetable spray; fill with vegetables. Place on a grill over medium heat. Grill until vegetables are crisp-tender. Remove vegetables to a serving bowl. Lightly drizzle with oil; add desired chopped herb and serve immediately. Serves 6.

Savory Beans & Tomatoes over Rice

This delicious side is just minutes away...packed with flavor and so satisfying!

4 to 6 slices bacon, diced
1 onion, diced
1 stalk celery, diced
1 T. garlic, chopped
14-1/2 oz. can diced tomatoes
2 15-1/2 oz. cans cannellini beans

hot pepper sauce and red pepper
   flakes to taste
1/8 t. Italian seasoning
2 to 3 T. butter
salt and pepper to taste
cooked rice

In a large skillet over medium heat, cook bacon until crisp. Remove bacon to a plate and keep warm, reserving drippings in pan. Sauté onion and celery in drippings until translucent. Stir in garlic and cook for 2 to 3 minutes. Add tomatoes with juice to onion mixture; bring to a simmer, stirring occasionally. Stir in beans with juice; return to a simmer. Add reserved bacon and remaining ingredients except rice; heat through. To serve, spoon over cooked rice. Serves 6 to 8.

Host a chuckwagon cookout. Set out hay bales for seating, then serve up ribs and burgers, baked beans and corn on the cob. Enamelware plates and colorful bandanna napkins complete the theme.

Savory Beans & Tomatoes over Rice

Lighter-Than-Air Potato Rolls

Lighter-Than-Air Potato Rolls

These rolls are wonderful right out of the oven, served with butter, jam, honey or apple butter.

1/2 c. instant mashed potato flakes   1/2 c. hot water
1 t. sugar   1/3 c. cold water
2 T. butter, softened   2 c. biscuit baking mix

In a bowl, stir together potato flakes, sugar, butter and hot water. Add cold water and baking mix; stir until a soft dough forms. Gently form dough into a ball on a floured surface; knead 8 to 10 times. Roll out into a 10-inch by 6-inch rectangle. Cut into 12 squares; arrange on an ungreased baking sheet. Bake at 450 degrees for about 10 minutes, until golden. Makes one dozen.

A roomy galvanized washtub makes a clever ice chest. Fill it up with ice, juice boxes, bottles of water or soda, and they'll stay frosty all day long.

Picnic Salad Skewers

What a fun way to eat a salad! For a meal-in-one version, slide on some cubes of salami and cheese too.

8 new redskin potatoes
8 pearl onions
1 green pepper, cut into 1-inch squares
1 red or yellow pepper, cut into 1-inch squares
16 cherry tomatoes

1 zucchini, sliced 1/4-inch thick
8 wooden skewers
8-oz. bottle favorite vinaigrette salad dressing
Optional: 4-oz. container crumbled feta cheese

Cover potatoes with water in a saucepan; bring to a boil over medium heat. Cook for 10 to 13 minutes, adding onions after 5 minutes; drain and cool. Thread vegetables alternately onto skewers. Arrange skewers in a large shallow plastic container. Drizzle with vinaigrette. Cover and refrigerate for at least one hour, turning frequently. Sprinkle with cheese at serving time, if desired. Makes 8 servings.

158

Need a quick snack to tide the kids over until dinnertime? Hand out little bags of crunchy snacks...just toss together cereal squares, raisins and a few chocolate-covered candies.

Picnic Salad Skewers

Orange-Melon Sunshine Salad

Orange-Melon Sunshine Salad

Try adding honeydew, cantaloupe or watermelon to this refreshing fruit salad.

2 c. orange juice
2 slices fresh ginger root

4 to 6 c. mixed melon balls
Garnish: fresh mint sprigs

Combine orange juice and ginger slices in a saucepan over medium heat. Bring to a boil; continue to boil until juice cooks down to 1/2 to 3/4 of its original amount. Remove from heat and discard ginger slices. Let cool. Arrange melon balls in a serving bowl; pour juice over top. Cover and chill for 2 hours to overnight. At serving time, stir gently to coat melon with juice; garnish with mint. Serves 4 to 6.

Sweet Ambrosia Salad

Kids of all ages love this sweet, creamy salad!

161

20-oz. can pineapple chunks, drained
14-1/2 oz. jar maraschino cherries, drained
11-oz. can mandarin oranges, drained

8-oz. container sour cream
10-1/2 oz. pkg. pastel mini marshmallows
1/2 c. sweetened flaked coconut

Combine fruit in a large bowl; stir in sour cream until coated. Fold in marshmallows and coconut; cover and chill overnight. Makes 8 to 10 servings.

Cool Summer Salad

A quick and tasty salad to pull together from your garden. It's great for potlucks and picnics because it travels well.

1 cucumber, sliced
2 to 3 tomatoes, diced
1/4 red onion, thinly sliced

1 avocado, halved, pitted and
  cubed
1/2 c. Italian salad dressing

Combine all vegetables in a bowl; drizzle salad dressing over top. Refrigerate, covered, for at least one hour. Toss gently before serving. Serves 4 to 6.

Use a plastic drinking straw to hull strawberries with ease. Just push the straw through the end without a stem and the leafy top will pop right off.

Cool Summer Salad

Fried Green Tomatoes

Fried Green Tomatoes

A summer delight! These crisp golden slices make yummy sandwiches too.

1 c. all-purpose flour
2 eggs, beaten
1 c. Italian-flavored dry bread
  crumbs
1/2 c. shortening

2 to 3 green tomatoes, sliced
  1/4-inch thick
Garnish: chipotle mayonnaise,
  crumbled feta cheese

Place flour, eggs and bread crumbs in separate small bowls. Melt shortening in a large skillet over medium heat. Dip each tomato slice into flour, then into eggs and lastly into bread crumbs. Add tomato slices to skillet and cook until golden, about 2 minutes on each side. Reduce heat to low; cook an additional 3 minutes, or until tender. Drizzle slices with chipotle mayonnaise; sprinkle with crumbled feta cheese. Serves 4 to 6.

Garlic fans will love the smoky flavor of garlic roasted on the grill.
Trim the top off a head of garlic and set it on a piece of aluminum foil.
Add olive oil and salt to taste. Wrap up well and grill over high heat
for about 30 minutes. Squeeze out the softened garlic onto crusty
bread...yum!

Cheddar-Dill Corn Muffins

With a little of this & a little of that, bake up a batch of delicious fresh muffins to go with barbecue or grilled chicken.

1 c. yellow cornmeal
1 c. all-purpose flour
1/3 c. sugar
2-1/2 t. baking powder
1/2 t. baking soda
1/4 t. salt
1 egg, beaten

3/4 c. milk
1-1/2 c. shredded sharp Cheddar
   cheese
1 c. corn, thawed if frozen
1/4 c. butter, melted
3 T. fresh dill, minced, or 1 T. dill
   weed

In a large bowl, mix cornmeal, flour, sugar, baking powder, baking soda and salt; set aside. In a separate bowl, whisk together egg and milk; stir in remaining ingredients. Add egg mixture to cornmeal mixture; stir just until moistened. Spoon batter into 12 greased or paper-lined muffin cups, filling 2/3 full. Bake at 400 degrees for about 20 minutes, until golden and a toothpick inserted in the center tests clean. Cool in pan on a wire rack for 10 minutes; turn muffins out of pan. Serve warm or at room temperature. Makes one dozen.

166

Kitchen shears are so handy for snipping fresh herbs and green onions...chop 'em right into the recipe.

Cheddar-Dill Corn Muffins

Quick Picnic Pickles

Quick Picnic Pickles

Jars of these fresh veggie pickles make great gifts to share with friends & neighbors.

1/2 c. rice vinegar
1/2 c. sugar
1-qt. wide-mouth canning jar and lid, sterilized
2 cucumbers, peeled and thinly sliced

1/2 red, orange or yellow pepper, cut into long strips
1/8 red onion, cut into wedges or strips
1 carrot, peeled and thinly sliced
1 T. fresh cilantro, chopped

Combine vinegar and sugar in canning jar; add lid and shake to mix well. Add vegetables and cilantro to jar in thin layers and pack to top. Fill jar with enough water to cover vegetables. Replace lid; seal tightly. Turn over jar to mix well. Refrigerate overnight before using. May keep refrigerated up to one week. Makes one jar; serves 6 to 8.

169

Going to a potluck cookout? Show off colorful bean salads and slaws by serving them in big one-gallon canning or pickle jars. Just wrap each jar in a napkin or tea towel to protect them on the way.

Classic Cookout Sides

Fresh Ranch Dressing

It's easy to make your own fresh salad dressing. Drizzle it over salads, spoon it over baked potatoes and serve as a veggie dip...yummy!

2 c. mayonnaise
1/2 c. milk
1-1/2 t. vinegar
1/4 t. Worcestershire sauce

1 green onion, finely chopped
1/3 c. grated Parmesan cheese
1/4 t. dill weed
1/8 t. pepper

Whisk together all ingredients in a large bowl. Pour into a large jar with a tight-fitting lid. Secure lid; keep refrigerated up to 2 weeks. Makes 4 cups.

Best Honey-Mustard Dressing

You'll love this dressing! It's terrific with chicken fingers and grilled chicken salad.

1 c. mayonnaise
3/4 c. sour cream

3/4 c. honey
3 T. mustard

170

Combine all ingredients; mix well and spoon into a covered container. Keep refrigerated up to 2 weeks. Makes about 2-1/2 cups.

No more soggy salads! Pour salad dressing in the bottom of your salad bowl, then add greens on top. Toss just before serving.

Fresh Ranch Dressing

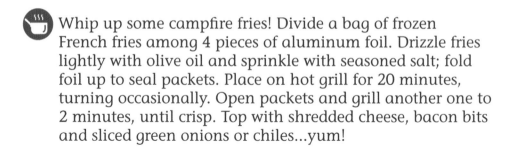

 Whip up some campfire fries! Divide a bag of frozen French fries among 4 pieces of aluminum foil. Drizzle fries lightly with olive oil and sprinkle with seasoned salt; fold foil up to seal packets. Place on hot grill for 20 minutes, turning occasionally. Open packets and grill another one to 2 minutes, until crisp. Top with shredded cheese, bacon bits and sliced green onions or chiles...yum!

Serve up a salad buffet for a warm-weather get-together with friends. Try a grilled chicken salad, a pasta salad, a crisp green tossed salad and a fruity gelatin salad. Crusty bread and a simple dessert complete a tasty, light meal.

Almost-instant herbed butter! Press a mixture of dried oregano, thyme, rosemary and a dash of garlic powder over a stick of chilled butter and slice. Delicious on warm rolls, or add a pat to a just-grilled steak.

When draining canned fruit, freeze the juice in ice cube trays...oh-so handy for adding a little sweetness to marinades and dressings.

Snackin' in the Shade

Strawberry-Watermelon Slush

A luscious combination of fresh summer fruit.

1 pt. strawberries, hulled and
   halved
2 c. watermelon, cubed and seeded

1/3 c. sugar
1/3 c. lemon juice
2 c. ice cubes

Combine all ingredients except ice cubes in a blender. Process until smooth. Gradually add ice and continue to blend. Serve immediately. Serves 5 to 6.

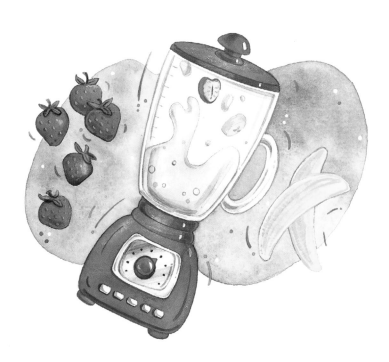

Whip up some fresh stirrers for lemonade and sweet tea! Simply thread melon balls or plump strawberries onto drinking straws.

Strawberry-Watermelon Slush

Grilled Pepperoni Log

Grilled Pepperoni Log

With a wonderful smoky taste, this recipe is a real crowd-pleaser!
It's easy to make too.

16-oz. loaf frozen bread dough, thawed
4-oz. pkg. sliced pepperoni

1 c. shredded mozzarella cheese
1/4 c. grated Parmesan cheese
1-1/2 t. Italian seasoning

Preheat grill until hot, about 375 degrees. On a lightly floured surface, roll out thawed bread dough into a 13-inch by 9-inch rectangle. Arrange pepperoni and cheeses evenly over dough. Sprinkle with seasoning. Roll up dough jelly-roll style, starting on one long edge; pinch seam to seal. Place dough seam-side down on grill over indirect heat. Cook for 20 minutes on each side. Slice to serve. Makes 12 to 14 servings.

Pizza Nibblers

Need something to munch on while dinner is on the grill? These little pizza-flavored nuggets are wonderful and just a little different!

20-oz. pkg. pretzel nuggets
1/2 c. oil

1 c. grated Parmesan cheese
1-1/4 oz. pkg. spaghetti sauce mix

Combine all ingredients in a large bowl; toss to coat nuggets well. Spread nuggets on an aluminum foil-lined baking sheet. Bake for 45 minutes at 275 degrees. Cool before serving. Makes 12 to 15 servings.

Yummy Campfire Cheese

Warm, melting cheese...a scrumptious taste treat to try at your next cookout!

8-oz. pkg. round Brie cheese   1 loaf crusty bread, torn
1 T. brandy or white grape juice

Set cheese in the center of a 12-inch piece of heavy-duty aluminum foil. Pierce top of cheese several times with a fork; sprinkle with brandy or juice. Seal foil tightly over cheese. Place foil packet on a grill over low heat, or hot campfire or fire pit coals. Cook, turning occasionally with tongs, for about 10 to 12 minutes, until cheese is soft and melted. Set packet on a heat-proof plate; open carefully. Serve with chunks of bread for scooping out warm cheese. Makes 4 to 6 servings.

178

Old-fashioned Mason jars make lovely lanterns for backyard gatherings! Nestle a tea light inside and hang with wire from tree branches or fenceposts. Citronella candles will keep mosquitoes away.

Yummy Campfire Cheese

Mari's Special Salsa

Mari's Special Salsa

It takes just a few minutes to stir up this fresh-tasting salsa...adjust the heat level to suit your own taste. Serve with tortilla chips or use it to sauce up grilled chicken breast.

2 14-1/2 oz. cans stewed tomatoes
4-oz. can chopped green chiles
3.8-oz. can chopped black olives, drained
1-1/4 c. hot or medium salsa
1 green pepper, finely chopped
1 red pepper, finely chopped

1 bunch green onions, very thinly sliced
1 T. olive oil
1 T. red wine vinegar
1/8 t. salt
1/8 t. pepper

Combine both cans of tomatoes and juice in a large serving bowl; chop up tomatoes with kitchen shears. Add chiles, olives, salsa, peppers and onions. Drizzle with oil and vinegar; season with salt and pepper. Stir all ingredients together. Cover and chill for a few hours or overnight to blend flavors. May be kept refrigerated up to 4 days. Makes about 7 cups.

181

Mild, medium or spicy...salsa is scrumptious on so many more foods than just tortilla chips and tacos. Try a spoonful of salsa as a topper for grilled chicken, fish, burgers, hot dogs or even baked potatoes.

Fresh-Squeezed Lemonade

There's nothing like homemade lemonade on a hot day...
and it's really so easy to make.

1-3/4 c. sugar
8 c. cold water, divided

6 to 8 lemons
Garnish: ice cubes, lemon slices

Combine sugar and one cup water in a small saucepan. Bring to a boil over medium-high heat; cook and stir until sugar dissolves. Cool to room temperature; chill. Juice lemons to measure 1-1/2 cups juice; remove seeds and strain pulp, if desired. In a large pitcher, stir together chilled syrup, lemon juice and remaining water. Chill for several hours to blend flavors. Serve over ice cubes; garnish with lemon slices. Makes 8 to 10 servings.

Fill up a relish tray with crunchy fresh cut-up veggies as a simple side dish. A creamy salad dressing can even do double duty as a veggie dip and a sandwich spread.

Fresh-Squeezed Lemonade

Robert's Corn Dip

Robert's Corn Dip

This dip is sooo delicious...a Gooseberry Patch favorite! The recipe makes enough to feed a crowd, yet it goes together in just minutes.

3 11-oz. cans sweet corn & diced
   peppers, drained
7-oz. can chopped green chiles
6-oz. can chopped jalapeño
   peppers, drained and liquid
   added to taste
1/2 c. green onion, chopped

1 c. sour cream
1 c. mayonnaise
1 t. pepper
1/2 t. garlic powder
16-oz. pkg. shredded sharp
   Cheddar cheese
scoop-type corn chips

In a large bowl, combine all ingredients except corn chips; mix well. Cover and refrigerate. Flavor is even better if made one to 2 days ahead of time. Serve with corn chips for scooping. Makes about 6 cups.

Herb Garden Dip

Serve with a big platter of colorful fresh vegetables... sure to be appreciated! For a lighter dip, just replace some of the sour cream with plain Greek yogurt.

1 c. sour cream
1/2 t. dried chives
1/2 t. dried parsley
1/2 t. dried marjoram
1/4 t. garlic powder
1/4 t. dried oregano

1/4 t. dried basil
1/8 t. dill weed
chips or crackers
assorted cut-up vegetables
   for dipping

Place sour cream in a small bowl and set aside. Crush together herbs; stir into sour cream and chill well. Serve with chips or crackers and fresh vegetables. Makes about one cup.

Zesty Black Bean Salsa

Enjoy with tortilla chips as a different take on salsa...spoon over grilled chicken or fish for a fresh new taste.

15-1/2 oz. can black beans,
  drained and rinsed
15-1/4 oz. can corn, drained
3/4 c. red pepper, diced
1/2 c. green onion, sliced

1/3 c. fresh cilantro, chopped
1/4 c. lime juice
1 t. ground cumin
tortilla chips

Combine beans, corn, pepper, onion and cilantro; mix well. In a separate bowl, whisk together lime juice, cumin and garlic salt; pour over bean mixture and toss gently. Makes 4 cups.

Scooped-out red and yellow peppers make fun containers for dips and sauces.

Zesty Black Bean Salsa

Sweet Salsa

Sweet Salsa

A fresh and fruity salsa that's sure to be a hit!

2 c. cantaloupe, peeled, seeded and
   finely chopped
2 c. cherry tomatoes, chopped
1/4 c. green onions, chopped
1/4 c. fresh basil, chopped
2 T. jalapeño peppers, diced

2 T. lime juice
2 T. orange juice
1/4 t. salt
1/8 t. pepper
tortilla chips

Stir together all ingredients except chips; cover and refrigerate for at least 30 minutes. Serve with chips. Makes about 4-3/4 cups.

Those who bring sunshine to the lives of others cannot
keep it from themselves.
-J.M. Barrie

Summertime Iced Tea

Freeze sprigs of fresh mint in ice cubes for a party-pretty touch.

4 c. boiling water
2 family-size tea bags
6 leaves fresh mint
6-oz. can frozen lemonade
    concentrate

1 c. sugar
5 c. cold water
Garnish: ice cubes, fresh mint
    sprigs

Pour boiling water into a large heatproof pitcher. Add tea bags and mint leaves; let stand for 5 minutes. Discard tea bags and mint leaves. Add frozen lemonade, sugar and cold water; mix well. Serve over ice, garnished with mint. Makes 8 to 10 servings.

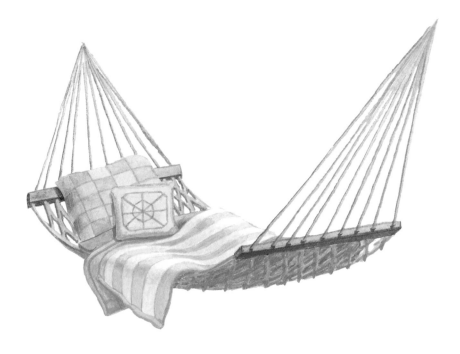

Use muffin tins to make giant ice cubes for party pitchers of lemonade and sweet tea...they'll last much longer than regular ice cubes!

Summertime Iced Tea

Mariachi Margarita Dip

Mariachi Margarita Dip

Turn any gathering into a fiesta with this sweet and sassy fruit dip.

8-oz. pkg. cream cheese, softened
1/3 c. frozen margarita drink mix,
   thawed
2 T. orange juice
1/4 c. powdered sugar

1/2 c. whipped cream
Garnish: lemon or lime wedge,
   sparkling sugar
assorted fruit slices and cubes

In a bowl, beat together cream cheese, margarita mix, orange juice and powdered sugar until smooth. Fold whipped cream into mixture until well blended. Cover and chill one hour. Moisten rim of a serving bowl with lemon or lime wedge. Quickly dip rim into sparkling sugar to coat. Spoon dip into bowl and serve with fruit. Serves 6 to 8.

When slicing apples and pears for a fruit platter, keep them from turning brown by soaking them in a mixture of one cup water and 2 tablespoons honey.

Snackin' in the Shade

Too-Good-to-Stop Spread

This blend of creamy cheeses and savory flavors is just delicious.

8-oz. pkg. cream cheese, softened
8-oz. pkg. crumbled feta cheese, softened
2 T. balsamic vinegar
1/2 c. sun-dried tomatoes in oil, drained, coarsely chopped and 1 T. oil reserved
1/2 c. kalamata olives cured in oil, drained and coarsely chopped
10 fresh basil leaves, thinly sliced and divided
bruschetta slices, garlic toast or flavored crackers

Blend together cheeses in a bowl; add vinegar. Stir in tomatoes, olives, reserved oil from tomatoes and half of the basil. Line a small bowl with plastic wrap; sprinkle with remaining basil. Pack cheese mixture into prepared bowl. Cover with more plastic wrap and refrigerate for one hour. At serving time, remove top piece of plastic wrap. Invert bowl onto a serving plate and peel off remaining plastic wrap. Serve with bruschetta slices, small slices of garlic toast or flavored crackers. Serves 8 to 10.

Roasted Red Pepper Spread

*You'll love this flavorful dip with all kinds of dippers!
It's a snap to make too.*

8-oz. container mayonnaise
8-oz. container sour cream
7-oz. jar roasted red peppers, drained and liquid reserved
salt and pepper to taste
1 handful fresh basil, loosely packed
salt and pepper to taste
Melba toast rounds, snack crackers, vegetable slices

In a food processor, combine mayonnaise and sour cream. Add peppers, basil, salt and pepper; pulse until well-combined. Blend in reserved liquid, one tablespoon at a time, to desired consistency. Spoon into a serving dish. Serve with Melba toast, crackers or vegetables. Makes 2 to 3 cups.

Too-Good-to-Stop Spread

Rosemary Lemon-Pineapple Punch

Rosemary Lemon-Pineapple Punch

So refreshing...just right for a garden party, reception or simply relaxing in the shade.

46-oz. can unsweetened pineapple
   juice
1-1/2 c. lemon juice
2 c. water

3/4 to 1 c. sugar, divided
4 to 5 sprigs fresh rosemary
1-ltr. bottle ginger ale, chilled

In a large saucepan, combine fruit juices, water, 3/4 cup sugar and rosemary sprigs. Bring to a boil over medium heat, stirring until sugar dissolves. Remove from heat; cover and let stand for 15 minutes. Discard rosemary; stir in more sugar to taste, if desired. Pour into a large pitcher; cover and chill. At serving time, add ginger ale; serve immediately. Makes 12 servings.

Keep bugs away from cool glasses of lemonade... simply poke a hole through a paper cupcake liner, add a straw, flip it upside-down and use it as a beverage cap. Clever!

Summer Sparkle

Serve in tall fluted glasses with plenty of ice...oh-so refreshing!

48-oz. bottle ruby red grapefruit
   juice
12-oz. can frozen orange juice
   concentrate, thawed
6-oz. can frozen lemonade
   concentrate, thawed

2-ltr. bottle lemon-lime soda,
   chilled
Optional: lemon slices, fresh mint
   sprigs

In a one-gallon pitcher, stir together all juices; cover and refrigerate until chilled. At serving time, add soda; garnish as desired. Serve immediately. Makes 16 to 20 servings.

Garnish cool beverages with fruit-flavored ice cubes. Cut favorite melons into cubes, purée in a food processor and freeze in ice cube trays.

Summer Sparkle

Cathy's Scotch Eggs

Snackin' in the Shade

Cathy's Scotch Eggs

A hearty appetizer for a hungry game-day crowd!

1 lb. ground pork sausage
2 T. dried parsley
1/2 t. dried sage
1/2 t. dried thyme
8 eggs, hard-boiled and peeled
1/2 c. all-purpose flour

1/2 t. salt
1/4 t. pepper
2 eggs, lightly beaten
1-1/2 c. dry bread crumbs
oil for frying
Garnish: favorite mustard

Combine sausage and herbs; mix well. Divide into 8 flattened patties. Cover each hard-boiled egg with a sausage patty, pressing to cover and seal. Combine flour, salt and pepper in a shallow bowl; place beaten eggs and bread crumbs in separate bowls. Roll eggs in flour mixture, then in beaten eggs and bread crumbs. Heat one inch of oil in a saucepan over medium-high heat. Cook eggs, a few at a time, in hot oil for 10 minutes, or until golden on all sides and sausage is no longer pink inside. Drain; cool and chill. Cut eggs into halves or quarters for serving; serve with mustard. Serves 8 to 10.

201

Classic Deviled Eggs

*You can't have too many deviled eggs at cookouts and picnics...
luckily, this recipe makes plenty!*

1 doz. eggs, hard-boiled, peeled
   and halved lengthwise
1/2 c. mayonnaise
2-1/2 T. sweet pickle relish

1 t. mustard
1/4 t. salt
1/8 t. pepper
Garnish: paprika

Separate hard-boiled egg yolks from egg whites; arrange egg whites on a serving plate and set aside. Mash egg yolks in a bowl; combine with remaining ingredients except paprika and mix well. Spoon yolk mixture into egg whites; sprinkle with paprika. Chill until serving time. Makes 2 dozen.

Just Peachy Cider

*A warming beverage for an Indian Summer bonfire cookout...
easily doubled for a crowd.*

4 5-1/2 oz. cans peach nectar   3/4 t. pumpkin pie spice
2 c. apple cider   4 slices orange

In a 3-quart slow cooker, combine nectar, cider and spice; top with orange slices. Cover and cook on low setting for 4 to 6 hours. Stir before serving. Serves 4.

On a cool evening, invite friends over to enjoy a warm mug and a crackling fire in the fire ring.

Just Peachy Cider

Sweet & Easy Iced Coffee

Sweet & Easy Iced Coffee

Just right for a steamy summer day...but we think you'll want to make it all year 'round!

1/2 c. sweetened condensed milk, divided

4 c. strong brewed coffee, cooled
ice cubes

Place 2 tablespoons of condensed milk into each of 4 tall glasses. Pour one cup of cooled coffee into each glass; stir to combine. Fill glasses with ice; stir to chill. Serves 4.

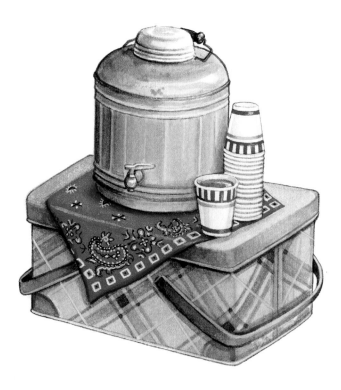

205

Freshen up a thermos in a jiffy. Spoon in a heaping teaspoon of baking soda, then fill with boiling water. Cap, shake gently and rinse...all ready to use again!

Pull-Apart Bacon Bread

A hearty burst of flavors...and so much fun to serve, monkey bread style!
Just pull off pieces to enjoy this savory appetizer.

1 to 2 t. oil
3/4 c. green pepper, diced
3/4 c. onion, diced
3 7-1/2 oz. tubes refrigerated
    buttermilk biscuits

1 lb. bacon, crisply cooked and
    crumbled
1/4 c. butter, melted
1 c. shredded Cheddar cheese

Heat oil in a large skillet; sauté green pepper and onion until tender.
Remove from heat; set aside. Cut biscuits into quarters; place in a bowl.
Add pepper mixture, bacon, butter and cheese; toss until mixed. Transfer
mixture to a greased 10" tube pan. Bake at 350 degrees for 30 minutes.
Invert onto a serving platter to serve. Serves 8.

Prepare crispy bacon easily. Place bacon slices on a broiler pan,
place the pan in a cool oven and turn the temperature to 400 degrees.
Bake for 12 to 15 minutes, turn slices over and bake for another 8 to
10 minutes.

Pull-Apart Bacon Bread

Sangria Punch

Snackin' in the Shade

Sangria Punch

So refreshing...try it with pink lemonade too. Perfect when you're making fajitas on the grill.

3/4 c. sweetened lemonade drink
  mix
4 c. cranberry juice cocktail
1 c. orange juice
1 T. lime juice

3 c. club soda, chilled
2 oranges, sliced
2 limes, sliced
Optional: maraschino cherries

Add drink mix to a large pitcher. Add fruit juices; stir until drink mix is completely dissolved. Cover and refrigerate until chilled. At serving time, stir in club soda and fruit. Makes 8 servings.

209

New plastic sand pails make whimsical party servers for chips and snacks. They're inexpensive, come in lots of bright colors and, perhaps best of all, stack easily so storage is a snap.

Cheddar-Bacon Balls

These tasty mini cheese balls can be whipped up ahead of the cookout and tucked in the fridge.

6 slices bacon, chopped
8-oz. pkg. Cheddar cheese, cubed
1/4 c. butter, cubed
2 T. fresh parsley, chopped
2 T. green onions, chopped

2 T. hot banana pepper rings
1/4 c. toasted pecans, finely
   chopped
assorted snack crackers

Cook bacon until crisp; drain, reserving one tablespoon drippings. In a blender or food processor, blend cheese, butter, parsley, green onions and pepper rings. Add bacon and reserved drippings; process until bacon is finely chopped. Chill mixture 3 hours, or until firm. Form mixture into one-inch balls. Roll balls in chopped pecans. Store in refrigerator up to 2 days before serving. Serve with crackers. Makes 2 dozen.

Stuffed Jalapeño Peppers

Cheese-filled poppers hot off the grill...anyone who likes spicy foods will love these!

2 doz. jalapeño peppers
8-oz. pkg. shredded Mexican
   blend cheese

1-lb. pkg. bacon

Slice jalapeños lengthwise without cutting all the way through; remove seeds and veins. Stuff with cheese; press closed. Cut bacon slices in half. Wrap a half-slice of bacon around each jalapeño and secure with a wooden toothpick. Grill over medium heat for 2 to 3 minutes on each side, until bacon is cooked and cheese is melted. Makes 2 dozen.

Cheddar-Bacon Balls

Brand-new terra-cotta pots make super summertime serving dishes. Line with a tea towel, napkin or bandanna and fill with flatware, straws, fresh veggies or bread sticks. You can even line one with plastic wrap and spoon in a creamy dip.

Freeze your own crystal-clear ice cubes for party pitchers. Bring a tea kettle of tap water to a boil. Let it cool to room temperature and pour into ice cube trays...or try muffin tins for super-size cubes! Pop ice cubes into a gallon-size plastic freezer bag until party time.

Make a warm batch of crostini to serve with a favorite spread. Thinly slice a loaf of French bread. Melt together 1/2 cup butter with 1/2 cup olive oil; brush over one side of each slice. Grill slices about 2 to 3 minutes per side, just until crisp and toasty.

Jelly jars make lovely lanterns for backyard gatherings. Nestle a tea light inside and hang with wire from tree branches or fenceposts. Look for citronella candles to keep mosquitoes away.

Backyard
Treats

Julie's Strawberry Yum-Yum

*A wonderful, light strawberry trifle that's a snap to put together...
this recipe is a winner!*

2 3.3-oz. pkgs. instant sugar-free
  white chocolate pudding mix
4 c. 1% milk
1 baked angel food cake, torn into
  bite-size pieces and divided
2 to 4 c. fresh strawberries, hulled,
  sliced and divided

2 8-oz. containers fat-free frozen
  whipped topping, thawed
10-oz. pkg. coconut macaroon
  cookies, crushed and divided

Combine dry pudding mix and milk in a large bowl. Beat with an electric
mixer on low speed for 2 minutes. Chill for a few minutes, until thickened.
In a large glass trifle bowl, layer half each of the cake pieces, pudding and
strawberries, one container whipped topping and half of the cookie crumbs.
Repeat layers, ending with cookies. Cover and chill until serving time.
Makes 8 to 10 servings.

214

Round out a cookout menu with a super-simple dessert. In parfait
glasses, layer cubes of pound cake with fresh peach slices and
whipped cream.

Julie's Strawberry Yum-Yum

Grilled Peaches

Grilled Peaches

A unique way to serve up one of summer's sweet natural delights.

4 peaches, halved and pitted
2 T. butter, melted
cinnamon to taste

8 scoops vanilla ice cream or
   frozen yogurt

Brush the cut side of each peach half lightly with butter. Place peaches cut-side down on a hot grill. Reduce heat and grill for 8 to 10 minutes, until tender. Remove to serving bowls. Sprinkle with cinnamon. Top with a scoop of ice cream or frozen yogurt. Serves 8.

Cinnamon Apples

Delicious with grilled sausage or pork chops, or spooned over ice cream for a luscious dessert.

8 to 10 Gala apples, cored
   and sliced
cinnamon to taste
1/2 c. brown sugar, packed

1/2 c. sugar
1/4 c. butter
1/2 c. honey
1 t. vanilla extract

217

Arrange apple slices in a 2-quart casserole dish; sprinkle with cinnamon and set aside. Combine sugars, butter and honey in a heavy saucepan over medium heat. Cook and stir until bubbly and sugars dissolve. Remove from heat; stir in vanilla and set aside. Pour sugar mixture over apples; stir gently until evenly coated. Cover with aluminum foil; bake at 400 degrees for 30 minutes, or until apples are tender. Makes 10 servings.

Fireside Banana Splits

You can't go wrong with this yummy recipe...it's always a hit!

6 to 8 bananas, unpeeled and
   stems removed
12-oz. pkg. semi-sweet chocolate
   chips

10-oz. pkg. mini marshmallows
Optional: salted peanuts

Lightly spray 6 to 8 pieces of aluminum foil with non-stick vegetable spray. Slice each banana peel lengthwise while also slicing the banana inside. Carefully open banana wide enough to sprinkle desired amount of chocolate chips and marshmallows inside. Add peanuts, if desired. Wrap filled bananas in foil. Place on a grill over high heat or directly in the coals of a campfire or fire pit. Grill for about 5 minutes, until chocolate and marshmallows are melted. Unwrap carefully; pull banana peels open. Makes 6 to 8 servings.

Did you know...you can shake up whipped cream in a Mason jar! Add one cup chilled whipping cream to a wide-mouth jar, close the lid tightly and shake vigorously for one to 2 minutes.

Fireside Banana Splits

Luscious Angel Cupcakes

Luscious Angel Cupcakes

Great to take to picnics or to a poolside party.

16-oz. pkg. angel food cake mix
3.4-oz. pkg instant vanilla pudding
  mix
2 8-oz. cans crushed pineapple

1 c. frozen whipped topping,
  thawed
2 c. assorted fresh berries

Prepare cake mix as directed on the package. Pour batter into 24 to 30 paper-lined muffin cups, filling each 2/3 full. Bake at 375 degrees for 12 to 15 minutes, until tops are golden and a toothpick tests clean. Cool cupcakes in pan for 10 minutes; remove to wire racks to cool completely. In a bowl, mix together dry pudding mix and undrained pineapple. Gently fold in whipped topping; spread evenly over cupcakes. Top cupcakes with berries; keep refrigerated until ready to serve. Makes 2 to 2-1/2 dozen.

Host an outdoor movie night in your own backyard! Great fun for watching the big game too. Call a local rental store for equipment, then choose your show. Sure to be a hit!

Just-for-Fun Fruit Pizza

Kids love to help make this delicious fruit pizza. Try your favorite berries as well as sliced kiwi and peaches. You can't go wrong!

8-oz. tube refrigerated crescent
   rolls
1 T. butter, melted
1/2 t. almond extract
4 t. sugar
3.4-oz. pkg. instant vanilla
   pudding mix

1 c. frozen whipped topping,
   thawed
1-1/2 c. milk
3 c. assorted berries and sliced
   fresh fruit

Unroll crescent rolls; do not separate. Press rolls into a ungreased 12" round pizza pan; press seams together. In a small bowl, combine butter and almond extract; brush over rolls. Sprinkle with sugar. Bake at 375 degrees for 11 to 13 minutes, until golden. Cool baked crust completely in pan on a wire rack. In a bowl, with an electric mixer on low speed, beat dry pudding mix and milk for one minute. Cover bowl and refrigerate for 10 minutes; fold in whipped topping. Spread pudding mixture evenly over crust. Arrange fruit over pudding. Cover and refrigerate for one to 3 hours; cut into wedges or squares. Makes 8 servings.

Round out a cookout menu with a super-simple dessert. In parfait glasses, layer cubes of pound cake with fresh peach slices and whipped cream.

Just-for-Fun Fruit Pizza

Golden Tequila Lime Tart

Golden Tequila Lime Tart

This fresh and summery tart is sure to be a winner at your next backyard cookout or Mexican feast!

12 graham crackers, coarsely
  crushed
1/4 c. pine nuts
3 T. sugar, divided
1/2 c. butter, melted
1/2 c. lime juice

1/4 c. gold tequila or lemon-lime
  soda
14-oz. can sweetened condensed
  milk
4 egg yolks
2 egg whites

Process crackers finely in a food processor. Measure 1-1/2 cups into a bowl; set aside. Finely process nuts and 2 tablespoons sugar; stir nut mixture and butter into crumbs. Press mixture evenly into the bottom and up the sides of an ungreased 9-1/2" round tart pan. In a large bowl, whisk together remaining ingredients except egg whites until well blended. In a separate large bowl, beat egg whites and remaining sugar with an electric mixer on high speed until soft peaks form. Add 1/4 of egg white mixture to milk mixture; gently fold in remaining mixture and spoon into crust. Bake at 325 degrees for 25 to 30 minutes, until center is set and edges of filling are puffed and light golden. Cool completely; chill for 2 hours. Serves 12.

Piña Colada Cake

A cool and refreshing dessert! Best served the same day it's made, before the cake gets soggy.

18-1/2 oz. pkg. yellow cake mix
15-oz. can cream of coconut
8-oz. can crushed pineapple,
  drained

2 c. frozen whipped topping,
  thawed
2 T. sweetened flaked coconut,
  toasted

Prepare cake mix according to package directions; bake in a greased 13"x9" baking pan. When cake has cooled, use a fork to poke holes in the top. Spread cream of coconut evenly over top of cake. Sprinkle with pineapple; spread whipped topping over entire surface. Sprinkle with coconut; chill. Makes 8 to 10 servings.

Caramel Apple Pie

Tender apples, ooey-gooey caramels, a nutty topping...
dessert doesn't get much better than this!

36 to 40 caramels, unwrapped
2 T. water
6 c. Granny Smith and/or Golden
   Delicious apples, peeled, cored
   and sliced
1 T. lemon juice
9-inch pie crust, unbaked

3/4 c. all-purpose flour
3 T. brown sugar, packed
1/2 t. cinnamon
1/2 t. nutmeg
1/4 t. salt
6 T. butter
1/2 c. chopped pecans

Combine caramels and water in the top of a double boiler. Cook and stir over low heat until caramels melt; remove from heat. Sprinkle apples with lemon juice. Layer apples in unbaked pie crust alternately with layers of melted caramel; set aside. In a separate bowl, combine flour, brown sugar, spices and salt. Cut in butter with a pastry blender; stir in pecans. Sprinkle mixture evenly over apples. Bake at 375 degrees for 40 minutes, or until golden and apples are tender. Serves 8.

Bake a favorite fruit crisp on the grill. Assemble ingredients in a cast-iron skillet. Preheat grill to medium-low and set skillet in the center. Grill, covered, for 15 to 20 minutes, until topping is golden and fruit filling is hot and bubbly. Delicious!

Caramel Apple Pie

Skillet S'Mores

Skillet S'Mores

Bored with s'mores? Surely not! This is another fun way to enjoy a chocolatey treat. Prepare it as soon as dinner is off the grill... it'll be cool by dessert time.

1 T. butter
10-oz. pkg. mini marshmallows
2 sleeves graham crackers, crushed

2 1-1/2 oz. chocolate candy bars, broken into pieces

Melt butter in a cast-iron skillet over a hot grill. Sprinkle in marshmallows; stir until completely melted. Remove from fire; stir in graham crackers and chocolate. Press into pan with the back of a spoon. Allow to cool completely; cut into wedges. Makes 10 servings.

229

A do-it-yourself sundae bar with several yummy choices of ice cream and toppings can double as both dessert and party fun.

Black Forest Brownie Sundaes

*Turn a packaged brownie mix into a delicious dessert
that's sure to impress.*

18-oz. pkg. brownie mix
21-oz. can cherry pie filling,
   divided
1/4 c. oil

2 eggs, beaten
1-1/4 c. semi-sweet chocolate chips
Garnish: vanilla ice cream

In a large bowl, mix together dry brownie mix, one cup pie filling, oil
and eggs. Pour into a greased 13"x9" baking pan. Bake at 350 degrees for
30 to 35 minutes, until firm. Sprinkle hot brownies with chocolate chips;
spread chips with a knife when melted. Let cool; cut into squares. Top
servings with a scoop of ice cream and a spoonful of the remaining pie
filling. Serves 8 to 12.

Now and then it's good to pause in our pursuit of happiness
and just be happy.
-Guillaume Apollinaire

Black Forest Brownie Sundaes

Joyce's Chocolate Chip Pie

Joyce's Chocolate Chip Pie

Chocolate, butter and whipped cream...oh, my!

3/4 c. mini semi-sweet
   chocolate chips
9-inch pie crust, unbaked
2 eggs, beaten
1/4 c. all-purpose flour
1/3 c. sugar

1-1/2 c. brown sugar, packed
1 c. chopped pecans
1/2 c. butter, melted and cooled
   slightly
Garnish: whipped cream, additional
   chocolate chips

Sprinkle chocolate chips in unbaked pie crust; set aside. In a bowl, combine remaining ingredients except garnish; stir until well blended. Pour egg mixture over chocolate chips in crust. Bake at 350 degrees for 30 minutes, or until golden. Pie will become firm as it cools. Garnish as desired. Serves 8.

Cookies & Cream
Ice Cream Squares

An all-time family favorite dessert...yummy and super-easy to make.

1/2 gal. vanilla ice cream
8-oz. container frozen whipped
   topping, thawed

18-oz. pkg. chocolate sandwich
   cookies, crushed

Place frozen ice cream in a large bowl; let stand at room temperature until softened. Fold whipped topping into ice cream; fold in crushed cookies. Spoon into a 13"x9" baking pan. Cover and freeze until firm. Cut into squares. Makes 12 to 15 servings.

Texas Sheet Cake

Round up your family & friends for this wonderful Texas-size cake.

1 c. butter
1 c. water
6 T. baking cocoa
2 c. all-purpose flour
2 c. sugar
1/2 t. cinnamon

1/2 t. salt
2 eggs, beaten
8-oz. container sour cream
1 t. baking soda
Garnish: chopped walnuts

Combine butter, water and cocoa in a saucepan over medium heat. Bring to a boil; stir well and remove from heat. In a bowl, mix flour, sugar, cinnamon and salt; stir into hot mixture. Combine remaining ingredients except nuts in a separate bowl; add to batter and mix well. Pour into a greased 15"x10" jelly-roll pan. Bake at 350 degrees for 22 minutes, or until cake tests done with a toothpick. Pour Chocolate Icing over cake while hot; sprinkle with nuts. Makes 20 servings.

Chocolate Icing:

1/2 c. butter
4 T. baking cocoa
6 T. milk

16-oz. pkg. powdered sugar
1 t. vanilla extract

Bring butter, cocoa and milk to a boil; remove from heat. Stir in powdered sugar and vanilla until smooth.

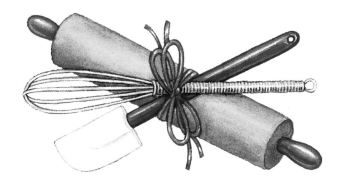

Texas Sheet Cake

Apple Blush Pie

Apple Blush Pie

This scrumptious pie can't be beat! Grandma's apple pie secret...
use a mix of apple types for great flavor.

2 9-inch pie crusts, unbaked
5 Granny Smith and/or Jonagold
   apples, peeled, cored and sliced
15-1/4 oz. can crushed pineapple

3/4 c. sugar
1/3 c. red cinnamon candies
2 T. instant tapioca, uncooked
3 T. butter, softened

Place one crust in a 9" pie plate; set aside. In a bowl, combine remaining ingredients except remaining crust; spoon into crust in pie plate. Cut remaining crust into 1/2-inch strips; form a lattice pattern over filling. Bake at 425 degrees for 10 minutes. Reduce temperature to 350 degrees and bake an additional 30 minutes. Let cool. Serves 8.

237

Old-fashioned games are terrific ice-breakers at cookouts.
Set up croquet or horseshoes for a fun activity while dinner
is on the grill.

Rustic Peach Tart

Oh-so easy to make...you'll want to try other fruit too!

9-inch pie crust, unbaked
3/4 c. plus 2 T. sugar, divided
1/3 c. all-purpose flour
1/2 t. ground ginger
1/4 t. nutmeg
16-oz. pkg. frozen sliced peaches

On a floured surface, roll out pie crust into a 12-inch circle. Place on an ungreased baking sheet and set aside. Mix 3/4 cup sugar, flour and spices; add frozen peach slices and toss to coat. Spoon peaches onto crust to within 2 inches of edge. Gently fold over edge of crust to form a 2-inch border, pleating as you go. Moisten crust edge with water; sprinkle with remaining sugar. Bake at 425 degrees until golden, about 15 minutes; reduce temperature to 350 degrees and bake until bubbly, about 30 to 35 minutes more. Makes 8 servings.

Slices of ripe watermelon are perfect for a simple dessert on a scorching day. To choose, tap a watermelon with your thumb and middle finger. If you hear a deep, low plunk the watermelon is ripe.

Rustic Peach Tart

Pineapple Sheet Cake

Backyard Treats

Pineapple Sheet Cake

Sheet cakes can't be beat for feeding a cookout crowd! This is a yummy alternative to the ever-popular chocolate variety.

2 c. all-purpose flour
2 c. sugar
2 t. baking soda
1 t. vanilla extract

2 eggs, beaten
20-oz. can crushed pineapple
Optional: chopped pecans

In a large bowl, combine flour, sugar, baking soda, vanilla, eggs and undrained pineapple. Mix well. Spread batter in a greased and floured 15"x10" jelly-roll pan. Bake at 325 degrees for 30 minutes, or until cake tests done with a toothpick. Spread with Cream Cheese Frosting while still warm. Sprinkle with pecans, if desired. Cool; cut into squares. Makes 15 servings.

Cream Cheese Frosting:

8-oz. pkg. cream cheese, softened
1/2 c. butter, softened

1 t. vanilla extract
1 c. powdered sugar

In a large bowl, blend all ingredients together until smooth.

Attach a strand of cool-burning light bulbs to the underside of a patio table umbrella to create a lantern effect.

Grilled Pineapple Sundaes

Luscious! Grilling really transforms slices of juicy ripe pineapple.

1/2 c. brown sugar, packed
2 T. butter, melted
2 T. lemon juice
1 t. cinnamon

1 pineapple, peeled, cored and
  sliced 1-inch thick
Garnish: vanilla ice cream, toasted
  coconut, maraschino cherries

In a bowl, mix brown sugar, butter, lemon juice and cinnamon in a bowl. Brush mixture over both sides of pineapple slices. Grill pineapple over high heat for about one minute on each side, until golden. Remove each slice to a dessert plate. Serve warm, topped with a scoop of ice cream, a sprinkle of coconut and a maraschino cherry. Serves 4 to 6.

"Deep-Fried" Ice Cream

A quick & easy no-fry version of the real thing...irresistible!.

4 c. bite-size crispy cinnamon rice
  cereal squares, lightly crushed
1 c. mini semi-sweet chocolate
  chips

2 pts. vanilla ice cream
1/2 lb. fresh strawberries, hulled
  and sliced
Garnish: honey, whipped cream

Combine cereal and chocolate chips in a bowl; set aside. Scoop 8 balls of ice cream with an ice cream scoop. Quickly roll ice cream balls in cereal mixture; mound in a 9" pie plate. Cover; freeze at least one hour until firm. At serving time, top ice cream balls with strawberries; drizzle with honey and dollop with whipped cream. Makes 8 servings.

Grilled Pineapple Sundaes

Super Berry Crisp

Super Berry Crisp

So easy to stir together...sure to be a hit!

21-oz. can cherry pie filling
2 c. fresh blueberries
1/4 c. butter
1/3 c. long-cooking oats, uncooked
1/3 c. all-purpose flour

1/4 c. brown sugar, packed
1 t. sugar
1/4 t. cinnamon
Garnish: whipped cream

Pour pie filling into an ungreased 9" pie plate; fold in blueberries and set aside. Melt butter in a small saucepan over medium-low heat. Add remaining ingredients except garnish to melted butter, stirring to coat well. Spread oat mixture over fruit in pie plate. Bake at 350 degrees for 35 minutes, or until topping is crisp and golden. Garnish individual servings with whipped cream. Serves 8.

No picnic table? No problem! Lay a length of plywood (or even an old door) across a couple of sawhorses and toss on a checkered tablecloth.

Grandma's Cherry Pudding Cake

*Garnish with a scoop of vanilla ice cream for
a luscious old-fashioned treat.*

1/4 c. butter, softened
2 c. sugar, divided
2 c. all-purpose flour
4 t. baking powder

1 c. milk
1 c. hot water
2 c. sour cherries, pitted

In a bowl, blend butter and one cup sugar; set aside. In a separate bowl, mix flour and baking powder. Add flour mixture and milk alternately to butter mixture. Stir until smooth; turn into a greased 8"x8" baking pan. In another bowl, mix remaining sugar, hot water and cherries. Pour over batter in pan; do not stir. Bake at 350 degrees for 40 minutes. Carefully remove pan from oven. Dessert will be thin on the bottom, with cherries and cake on top. As it cools, bottom layer will thicken into a sauce. Serve warm, scooping out cake and spooning some sauce over top. Serves 9.

246

Make a luscious sauce for pound cake...simply purée fruit preserves
with a few tablespoons of fruit juice.

Grandma's Cherry Pudding Cake

Coconut Cream Pie

Coconut Cream Pie

An old favorite! Spreading meringue so it touches the edges of the pie crust is the secret to keep it from shrinking...works every time!

3/4 c. sugar, divided
1/2 t. salt
3 T. cornstarch
2-1/2 c. whole milk
3 eggs, separated

1 t. vanilla extract
1 T. butter, melted
3/4 c. sweetened flaked coconut
9-inch pie crust, baked

In a saucepan over medium-low heat, combine 1/2 cup sugar, salt, cornstarch and milk. Cook, stirring often, until slightly thickened. Place egg yolks in a bowl. Pour 1/4 cup of milk mixture into yolks; beat until well combined. Transfer yolk mixture back to milk mixture; cook and stir for about 2 minutes, until thickened. Stir in vanilla, butter and coconut; pour into pie crust. Set aside to cool. In a bowl, beat together egg whites and remaining sugar with an electric mixer on high speed until stiff peaks form. Spoon meringue over cooled pie, spreading to the edges. Bake at 425 degrees for about 5 minutes, until meringue is golden. Serves 8.

249

Banana Supreme Pie

Shh...don't tell anyone how easy it is to make this delectable pie.

3.4-oz. pkg. instant vanilla
    pudding mix
1/2 c. milk
1 c. sour cream

12-oz. container frozen whipped
    topping, thawed
1 to 2 ripe bananas, sliced
9-inch graham cracker crust

In a large bowl, combine dry pudding mix, milk, sour cream and whipped topping; stir very well and set aside. Arrange banana slices in bottom of pie crust. Spoon pudding mixture over bananas; cover and chill until serving time. Makes 6 servings.

Tropical Carrot Cake

An irresistible dessert perfect for a springtime get-together.

18-oz. pkg. carrot cake mix
1/2 c. water
1/2 c. oil
4 eggs, beaten
8-oz. can crushed pineapple

1/2 c. chopped nuts
1/2 c. sweetened flaked coconut
1/2 c. raisins
16-oz. container cream cheese
   frosting

In a bowl, combine dry cake mix, water, oil, eggs and pineapple with juice.
Beat with an electric mixer on medium speed for 2 minutes. Stir in nuts,
coconut and raisins. Grease and flour the bottoms only of two, 8" round
cake pans. Pour batter into pans. Bake at 350 degrees for 30 to 35 minutes,
until a toothpick inserted in center comes out clean. Cool layers in pans
10 minutes. Remove to a wire rack to cool completely. Fill layers and frost
with frosting. Makes 12 servings.

A tray of mini potted herbs makes a sweet centerpiece...afterwards,
send them home with guests as parting gifts.

Tropical Carrot Cake

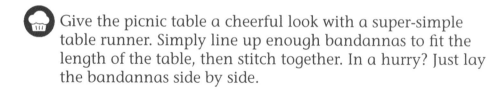

Give the picnic table a cheerful look with a super-simple table runner. Simply line up enough bandannas to fit the length of the table, then stitch together. In a hurry? Just lay the bandannas side by side.

Dip the tops of ice cream cones in melted chocolate, then roll in candy sprinkles. Filled with scoops of ice cream, these cones make any treat extra special.

Paper plates and cups don't have to be boring. Look for brightly colored ones, then quickly dress them up with stickers or rubber stamps.

Try making s'mores with chocolate graham crackers, toasted marshmallows and mini peanut butter cups... yummy!

Index

Index